THE QUOTA QUESTION

RESERVATION REDEFINED

UJJAY

Made with ♥ on the Notion Press Platform
www.notionpress.com

Contents

About The Author

Ujjay, a dedicated law student in his final year, is passionate about legal studies and committed to making legal knowledge accessible to all. As the founder of the Instagram handle **"nattylawyer,"** he has actively shared insights on various legal topics through engaging blogs. Inspired by the maxim "ignorantia juris non excusat,", Ujjay strives to empower individuals through legal awareness and education.

Preface

India, a nation renowned for its rich cultural tapestry, has grappled with the legacy of the caste system, a hierarchical social structure that has perpetuated inequality for centuries. In response to these historical injustices and with the aim of fostering a more equitable society, the Indian government implemented a system of reservations, a form of affirmative action designed to uplift disadvantaged communities. The implementation of reservations has extended across various sectors, including education and public employment. It mandates the reservation of a specific proportion of seats in educational institutions and government jobs for individuals belonging to these designated categories. While the intention behind this policy is laudable, its implementation has sparked considerable debate and controversy.

Critics argue that the reservation system, while well-intentioned, has led to unintended consequences such as a decline in meritocracy and a sense of entitlement among beneficiaries. They contend that it may inadvertently perpetuate the very social divisions it seeks to eradicate.

Conversely, proponents of the reservation system maintain that it is a necessary measure to rectify historical injustices and ensure social justice. They argue that it provides a level playing field for marginalized communities, enabling them to access education and employment opportunities that were previously denied to them.

The ongoing debate surrounding the reservation system underscores the complex interplay of social, economic, and political factors at play. As India continues to evolve, it is imperative to strike a balance between affirmative action and meritocracy, ensuring that the benefits of economic growth are shared equitably across all segments of society. This book embarks on an in-depth exploration of this multifaceted policy, delving into its historical roots, legal framework, and contemporary debates.

We begin our journey by tracing the origins of the caste system, examining its rigid social hierarchy and how it has impacted the lives of millions across generations. We then explore the seeds of reservation sown in pre-independent India, highlighting the early movements and leaders who advocated for social justice and equality. Following this historical grounding, we turn our focus to the specific case of Tamil Nadu, a state with a unique history of reservation and social reform movements. We will analyze how the reservation system in Tamil Nadu differs from other Indian states, providing a comparative perspective.

Moving forward, the book delves into the core questions surrounding reservation. We will explore the rationale behind its implementation, examining arguments for and against its continued existence. The path of reservation will be traced, highlighting its evolution through constitutional provisions and landmark legal battles. We will also pay tribute to the leaders who were instrumental in securing this historic victory for marginalized communities. One of the most pressing contemporary debates surrounding reservation canters around the question of "how long?" This book will engage with this crucial question, analysing arguments about the continued necessity of affirmative action in contemporary India.

The recent emergence of casteless certificates and their impact on the reservation system will also be addressed. This emerging trend raises intriguing questions about social mobility and the potential for change within the social fabric of Indian society.

Ultimately, this book aims to illuminate the complexities of reservation, through this journey, we hope to shed light on how reservation has played a role in fostering a more equitable and inclusive society. Join us as we delve into the intricacies of this critical policy, navigating the debates and challenges that lie ahead.

CHAPTER ONE

ORIGIN AND BACKGROUND OF CASTE SYSTEM

The caste system in India is a complex and deeply ingrained part of the country's social and historical identity. There are different theories on the origin of the caste system in India. Before getting into the concept of the origin let's take a quick look on the etymology of the word **'Caste'**. The word caste derived from the **Spanish; Portuguese** *"Casta"* means *Race*. Hereditary Indian social groups called it *Jathi* which rooted to the word *Jana* which implies 'taking birth'.

1.1 THEORETICAL ORIGINS

The traditional theory says that the caste is of **Divine Origin**, it is an extension of the *Varnasystem*. According to this the system is created from the body of Brahma. At the apex of the social hierarchy were the **Brahmins**, who primarily served as teachers and intellectuals, they originated from **Brahma's head**. Next in line were the **Kshatriyas**, representing warriors and rulers, who were believed to have emerged from Brahma's arms. The **Vaishyas**, associated with trade and commerce, were created from his thighs. Occupying the lowest rung were the **Shudras**, who were said to have come from Brahma's feet. The symbolism behind these origins is profound: the mouth, associated with preaching and learning, corresponds to the Brahmins; the arms, signifying protection, align with the Kshatriyas; the thighs, symbolizing cultivation and business, pertain to the Vaishyas; and the feet, supporting the entire body, represent the duty of the Shudras—to serve the other three varnas. Over time, intermarriages between these four varnas led to the emergence of various **sub-castes.**

In light of *socio-historical theory,* the caste system in India has its roots in the arrival of the Aryans around 1500 BCE. As the Aryans entered India, they disregarded local cultures and embarked on a process of conquest and control in the northern regions. Simultaneously, they pushed the indigenous people southwards or into the jungles and mountainous areas of northern India. The Aryans had themselves classified as **Rajanyas,** the warriors (later renamed as Kshatriyas), Brahmanas, the priest, the Vaishiyas, the farmers and craftsman. There were also servants of two types and they were called Sudras. One was of the locals who were subdued by the Aryans and the other was the descendant of Aryans with locals.

The *occupational theory* says that in India, as in many other societies worldwide, the tradition of occupational inheritance prevailed. Sons followed in their fathers' footsteps, inheriting their family's profession. Over time, these families grew larger and evolved into distinct communities, known as Jatis. Families sharing the same profession formed social bonds and organized themselves into cohesive communities based on their common occupation.

1.2 BACKGROUND OF CASTE SYSTEM

Social structure is a complex web that binds various institutions, associations, and groups into a system of organizational and functional interdependence. In rural areas, caste is a crucial component of this structure. Stratification refers to the hierarchical ranking of society's members based on the unequal distribution of valued rewards such as wealth, prestige, and power. It is a universal aspect of all societies. The concept that a society with genuine equality among its members is a myth that has never been realized throughout human history.

While the forms and proportions of stratification may differ, its essence remains constant. India presents a unique system of social stratification based on birth, unlike any other in the world. No matter how distinguished an individual may become, they are intrinsically linked to the caste they were born into, with no separate identity apart from it. Caste system entails number of characteristics in it.

- **Segmental Division:** The caste system is characterized by the autonomy of each caste, functioning as independent entities from one another. Membership in a caste is determined by birth, making it immutable. Consequently, individuals cannot transition from one caste to another. Each caste possesses its distinct lifestyle, governed by its own set of rules and regulations, customs, traditions, practices, and rituals. Each caste has its governing body known as the caste council, responsible for enforcing these rules. Thus, each caste operates as a separate social microosm
- **Hierarchy:** The caste system is inherently hierarchical, comprising four primary varnas or castes, listed in descending order of rank: Brahmins, Kshatriyas, Vaishyas, and Shudras. Numerous castes exist between the two extremes of Brahmins and Shudras, with their social status largely determined by their proximity to the Brahmins. This hierarchy is a defining feature of the caste system, highlighting the unequal distribution of social status and power among different castes.
- **Endogamy:** Endogamy refers to the practice of marrying within one's own caste. This principle dictates that members are strictly prohibited from marrying outside their caste. Violating the rule of endogamy can lead to ostracism and loss of caste status. Moreover, marriage within the same Gotra or clan is forbidden, enforcing a rule of exogamy. This rule is particularly adhered to in rural settings. However, there are notable exceptions to the rule of endogamy, including anuloma and pratiloma marriages.
- **Fixity of Occupation:** The caste system is also defined by the fixed nature of occupations. These occupations are hereditary, meaning that members of a caste are expected to follow the traditional occupation of their forebears without deviation. For instance, Brahmins traditionally perform religious ceremonies, while washermen see it as their duty to launder clothes for others. However, certain occupations like trade, agriculture, and military service are regarded as open to all, irrespective of caste.
- **Commensality:** Commensality refers to the beliefs, practices, rules, and regulations governing inter-caste relationships, particularly concerning the types of food and water consumed. Members of a caste will only accept 'food' (uncooked food) from their own caste or from castes that are ritually higher. Additionally, there are specific restrictions on accepting water from members of different castes. For example,

Brahmins abstain from eating certain foods like onions, garlic, cabbage, carrots, and beetroot. Consumption of beef is strictly forbidden except for those considered untouchables. Caste members also observe strict rules regarding social interactions. Some castes are considered polluting by touch, hence labelled as 'untouchables. In Kerala, for instance, a Nayar can approach a Nambudri Brahmin but must avoid physical contact

- **Purity and Pollution**: The caste system is deeply rooted in the concepts of purity and pollution. These concepts are crucial in determining the hierarchical position of a caste or sub-caste. Brahmins are deemed the purest, occupying the highest rank in the caste hierarchy, while Harijans, not included in the Varna system, are considered the most polluting and occupy the lowest rank.

- **Unique Culture**: "Castes are small, complete social worlds in themselves, distinctly separated yet existing within the larger society." Each caste has a unique culture, customs, and traditions that distinguish it from other castes. These include specific food habits, occupational specializations, and behavioural patterns, which are passed down through generations via socialization.

- **Caste Panchayat**: The Caste Panchayat is responsible for enforcing the code and discipline within the caste. It handles issues like breach of marriage promises, adultery, illicit relations with members of other castes, cow killing, insulting Brahmins, and non-payment of debts. The Panchayat imposes various punishments, ranging from hosting a dinner for fellow caste members to paying fines, undergoing purification ceremonies, performing pilgrimages, or facing segregation.

- **Closed Group**: Caste is a closed group due to its practices of endogamy, fixed occupations, hereditary roles, and unique culture. Max Weber described caste as "a closed status group" because the obligations and barriers inherent in such a group are intensified within a caste.

- **Civil and Religious Disabilities**: Lower castes often face numerous civil, social, and religious disabilities. They are typically required to live on the outskirts of villages and are denied access to places of worship, cremation grounds, schools, public roads, and hotels. Even the touch or shadow of lower caste members can defile individuals of higher castes. In Kerala, a Nambudiri Brahmin must avoid the touch of a Nayar and maintain a distance of thirty-six feet from a Thiya caste member and ninety-six feet from a Pulyan caste member to avoid defilement.

- **Rooted in the Divine Plan:** The caste system is believed to have been ordained by God and is supported by religious doctrines. It is based on the doctrine of Karma and the theory of rebirth, giving it a divine justification.

CHAPTER TWO

DO CASTE SYSTEM STILL EXSISTS?

We are here to discover about reservation in India, but what makes it essential to know about, is the caste system still prevail? It's modern India in 21'st century. Do we still see the existence of the castes among people? I live in an urban area. I don't see any people here talking or asking about their caste, no bragging about caste pride! What makes it indispensable?

Also, here comes another decisive question: Is the caste system exclusive to Hinduism or endemic only to India? Before jumping into the answers of those questions let's try to look at our surroundings, take a newspaper, get into a talk with elders of the family, or walk to someone who you don't know, the immediate inquiry after you get to know a little is "what is your native? "" what language do you speak in your home?" "What is your family deity?". If you are in a rural area, the next question would be "Which Street do you live in?" What does your dad do or your grandparents did? Is the occupation they did is your family occupation? When you still continue the conversation, the inquiry would still extend like getting to know about the common friend, or known bigshot of the street or the village, knowing your peer groups, asking about the relatives that they would probably know by friend of friend or kin.

After a serious inquisition, one would actually come to a conclusion of what caste you would probably belong to. Here, nobody directly asked you "Hey! What caste you belong to?" but actually they indirectly concluded it. At Least once in life we would have been in a situation to answer those questions. This itself gets us to the answer of the very first question "Do **caste systems still exist?".**

Firstly, let's talk about the castes in India, there are about 3,000 castes and 25,000 subcastes in India. Digging deeper, as we have already seen in the origin of the caste, literary texts and many textbooks says caste system came to India by **Vedic age,** the 4 Vedas explains about the **Varna system.** Also, in the holy book of Hinduism **Bhagavad Gita**, Krishna says that he is the one who created this varna system on the basis of one's *Karma and nature.* [Chapter 18, verse 41]. Also, there are people who heat up the debate that the caste system existed even before the Aryan, they also criticize that the caste system existed in Dravidian India.

But looking into the *Sangam literature,* there existed only a classification of people but what worthy to note is that people were not discriminated against, also the classification was not by birth but by the geographical region one lives in. People lived in 5 different geographical regions [*Kurinji,Mullai,Marutham,Neithal,Paalai]* and were classified based on it; there was no restriction or discrimination, as in the varna system.

Secondly, coming to the question of Caste existence, one cannot deny its existence and discrimination based on it prevails even in today's modern India. According to the National Crime Records Bureau, out of the total number of murders, honour killing is a significant reason for it. There are several other incidents we can see in our daily life.

And finally, when, addressing the caste system, in a narrow view it only talks about Hinduism and India, but in a broader sense subcastes also exist in other religions and in other nations as well. However, the Indian caste system is notably rigid with very limited social mobility, while class systems allow for greater mobility based on personal achievements, Caste is determined by birth, whereas class can be influenced by education, occupation, and wealth. The caste system has intricate rules about purity, pollution, and social interactions, which are less pronounced in other systems.

CHAPTER THREE

WHO ARE DOWN-TRODDEN?

As we have seen the origin and existence of the caste system in India, we have to answer this very essential and interesting question: "who are downtrodden?", "What makes them downtrodden?"," What makes the caste system involved in it?" . Before getting answers one common question that arises is "what makes reservation important and what does the caste system deal with? "

As we have seen earlier: **"While the caste system and reservation policies are specific to India, the issue of discrimination exists in other countries as well."**

Firstly, it is crucial to recognize that reservation in India isn't solely for the so-called lower castes within the caste hierarchy. It also extends to individuals who face economic, political, and social discrimination. Thus, these discriminated people of the society are the downtrodden.

3.1 POLITICALLY DOWNTRODDEN:

The downtrodden in India's caste system refer to those who have historically faced marginalization due to their position in the hierarchical caste structure. In Political aspect, downtrodden are the people of the society who grapple with discrimination on multiple fronts: **powerlessness, denial of fundamental rights, mistreatment, and the inability to voice** their concerns or challenge the ruling elite. They could not participate in any political process or decisions and had no political voice.

Historically in India, the Brahmins, as the highest caste or varna, held significant influence. They provided guidance to the Kshatriyas, who were warriors and aristocrats. In turn, the Kshatriyas exerted control over the Vaishyas (businesspeople) and the Sudras (labourers). Interestingly, even within the so-called Upper caste, there existed oppression within the caste hierarchy. Thus, the wealthy Vaishyas who oppress Sudras were downtrodden by the Kshatriyas, and the Kshatriyas that rule the country is downtrodden by the Brahmins. Also, there was gender inequality, Women of any caste were oppressed by the men of their caste also the upper caste.

3.2 SOCIALLY DOWNTRODDEN:

The socially downtrodden are those who have endured severe oppression at the hands of the upper castes. They were systematically denied educational opportunities due to discrimination based on birth. The cruel ideology perpetuated by the upper castes labelled these individuals as impure and unworthy of education, stripping them of their dignity. These socially downtrodden individuals faced not only educational deprivation but also systematic mistreatment. They were barred from entering religious places, deemed impure by the upper castes. Moreover, they were forbidden from walking or speaking freely in the presence of those higher in the caste hierarchy. They were tagged as **Untouchables,** and were discriminated against based on birth, they were denied their rights such as what job they can do, where they can live. These are faced by almost more than half of the people in society, people exploited by every upper class in the hierarchy.

Despite the remedial efforts initiated in post-colonial India, the ancient social institution of untouchability can still be seen in some parts of society.

3.3 ECONOMICALLY DOWNTRODDEN:

Over thousands of years, lower caste people like Sudras, Vaishyas were not allowed to own land or other properties. These people were the working class, who were humiliated and exploited by the upper castes. They toiled for long hours, yet their wages remained insufficient. Denied property ownership and subjugated by the upper caste, they endured exploitation and disrespect. Their economic isolation did not result from crop failure or production losses, but rather from the inequitable distribution of wealth.

Thus, **downtrodden people are not just one caste of society, they are people of constructed identity.** While it's important to understand that those who perpetuate caste pride and discriminate against lower castes may have themselves faced discrimination from upper castes in the past, this doesn't excuse their current actions

CHAPTER FOUR

DISCRIMINATION IN THE NAME OF CASTE

Over a period of years, people were discriminated against by birth, this was socially prevailed, and which made them economically and politically downtrodden. In India this existed in the name of caste and religious practice. While viewing the discrimination of caste we look at this from its very origin.

*In Ancient India, the Varna system, unlike the slavery system, people were termed as **polluted, ritually impure.** They were **segregated and marginalized** from the rest of society. Their social interaction with other castes was **highly restricted.** They were often relegated to **menial and degrading jobs,** such as cleaning, sweeping, and handling animal carcasses and human waste. They were **not allowed to enter temples.** They were **denied access to the same water sources** as higher-caste individuals. Their touch was considered **polluting.** They faced **severe social and economic marginalization.** They were not allowed to get education.*

*Later, in the British colonial rule, the lives of oppressed and lower castes were profoundly impacted. Higher castes were given senior administrative jobs while the lower castes were denied access to basic health care and education. They were often shunned entirely from society, relegated to jobs considered unclean such as water disposal, toilet cleaning and cremation. The social categories of religion and castes that we see today were developed during the British rule. Since information was scarce and the colonizers held absolute power over information. The British elevated selected Brahminic Sanskrit texts like **Manusmriti** to canonical status adding the supposed origin of caste in the Rig Veda. These categories were institutionalized through the census in the mid to late 19th century, simplifying and standardizing the caste system.*

Now, what is widely accepted as Hinduism was in fact an ideology better called Brahmanism. During colonial rule, one's social identity could change easily as moving from one village to another. The British administration influenced the fluidity of social roles and identities.

Let us now look at the multifaceted discrimination in the contemporary India:

When discussing about the discrimination, let us consider some key topics: **literacy, economic development, employment and occupation, political representation, violence against and crimes committed.**

4.1 LITERACY:

Discrimination in education remains a significant issue in India, affecting various marginalized groups. Education is an important tool for the development of the people, but caste-based discrimination affects it. In schools across India, discrimination persists, particularly affecting students from scheduled castes. These students are sometimes excluded from activities and interactions with students from other communities. Unfortunately, some teachers exhibit disinterest in supporting scheduled caste students, assuming that these children have limited prospects and will eventually engage in traditional, caste-based occupations.

Various caste-based discrimination is found in rural government schools where lower caste students face discrimination for their caste. Mid-day meal scheme are introduced to boost education and nutritional standards of the marginalized and economically weaker sections but students are discriminated against by sitting separately from higher castes, Higher caste students often reject food prepared by scheduled caste individuals, leading them to avoid eating meals at school and instead go home. In Rajasthan, Valmiki community students' plate is not washed by the helpers who wash upper castes plates. In the village they are not allowed to drink water directly from the pot, they need someone to pour water from a distance. According to a report by Indian Dalit Solidarity Network, the dropout rate of Dalit children is 51% while national average is 37%. Also, in school out of 14 cases of violence reported ,12 cases are about sexual abuse of children from a marginalized community, and also higher numbers of student's dropouts and suicides are results of bullying them in the esteemed institutions. Elite Indian universities have long been criticized for practicing caste-based discrimination. According to government higher education data, the enrolment of students from marginalized communities *(such as Scheduled Castes or SCs) in 2019-20 was **14.7%** of all students aged 18-23. Over the last five years, more than **19,000 SC, ST, and Other Backward Classes students** have been excluded from the education stream in Indian Institutes of Technology (IITs), Indian Institutes of Management (IIMs), and central universities across the country.*

4.2 ECONOMIC DEVELOPMENT:

*India's journey since independence has been marked by significant economic growth. Over the past two decades, the nation has experienced sustained GDP growth, averaging around 7% annually. India's economic progress has not translated equally for all citizens. Over **90%** of workers remain employed in the informal sector, lacking employment security and benefits. Despite lifting millions out of poverty, India still has **350 million people** living below the poverty line. This economic disparity is mainly due to lack of education, and lack of opportunity. Discrimination based on caste leads to inefficiencies in resource allocation. As a result, economic growth is hindered, and opportunities are not equally accessible to all. Researches have shown that Scheduled castes and Scheduled tribes face significant disparities in income and status in the urban labour market. The private sector may not be entirely free of discrimination, and human capital differences alone do not explain the lack of advancement among lower castes.*

4.3 EMPLOYMENT AND OCCUPATION:

*The Indian government has taken affirmative actions for equal opportunity and to improve the status and living conditions of the oppressed people. Research found that discrimination in **employment and wages** is significantly higher in the **private sector** compared to the public sector. This discrimination leads to **reduced wage income**, exacerbating poverty among the discriminated group. occupational **discrimination** (unequal access to jobs) plays a more critical role than **wage discrimination** (unequal pay for the same job). Subsequent studies using the National Sample Survey (NSS) data on employment and unemployment found that **caste-based wage discrimination** accounted for **21% to 40%** of the wage gap among **regular workers**. However, this discrimination was negligible for casual and informal sector workers. Among **regular salaried workers**, about **18%** of Scheduled Castes (SCs) reported **discrimination in selection**. Approximately **22%** reported that **high-caste employers** gave* *preference to individuals of their own caste during employment. Around **23%** mentioned that **high-caste persons** were selected with **less qualification.** Even in many governments esteemed institutions, the issue of caste-based representation in faculty hiring is a topic of concern, it is identified that these institutions had not been implementing reservation in its entirety. According to data from the HRD Ministry in December 2018: SCs, STs, and OBCs together made up just 9% of total faculty in IITs. In IIMs, the representation was even lower, with only 6% of faculty coming from these categories.*

4.4 VIOLENCE AND CRIMES:

The incidents of hate crimes based on castes and attacks are frequently witnessed, as per statistics provided by NCRB report crimes against Scheduled castes have increased by 1.2%in 2021.Uttar Pradesh reported the highest number of cases, further, crimes against Scheduled tribes have increased by 6.4% in 2021.Madhya Pradesh reported the highest number of cases. Incidents like Dalit minor attacks, gangrapes, treating them as impure and unholy, assaults and violence are high in number; The reports also show that violence against Dalit women has also increased. Studies of hate crimes in India show that they have steadily risen over the past five year. The more common hate crimes, they found, were honor killings and 'cow-related violence', that was rare earlier but has become more frequent over the past five years. Honor killing in India is becoming so common, the National Crime Records Bureau (NCRB) reported 25 honor killings each in 2019 and 2020, and 33 in 2021.Most honor killings target women.

The concept of women as bearers of family reputation plays a significant role in perpetuating this crime. The DHRHNet, along with the National Council for Women Leaders (NCWL), recently published a report on caste-based honor killings from seven states: Haryana, Gujarat, Bihar, Rajasthan, Tamil Nadu, Maharashtra, and Uttar Pradesh top it.

CHAPTER FIVE

LEGAL PROVISIONS

As we have seen from the very beginning, caste system in India is uprooted and existing for several hundred years, also we have seen how it still prevails in the modern India. We have seen how people were discriminated in the past and how discrimination itself evolved in modern times. We also saw the different aspects of society that makes people downtrodden. After reading all the above topics you would have probably get few questions:

1.If discrimination in the society on the basis of caste is a problem, is it that the discrimination based on caste should be eliminated or the caste itself should be eliminated.

2.If caste itself is a problem, as it discriminates against people, reservation also discriminates against people, so what is the actual purpose of the reservation?

3.How reservation brings equality?

4.Are all reservations based on caste? Does caste alone discriminate against people? If there are other grounds on which people are discriminated against, does reservation also apply for them?

Let us find answers and understand reservation and caste in legal aspects in this passage.

The need for equality in the society brings reservation, but why do we need Equality? What is equality? Equality explains that individuals should not be discriminated against on the basis of race, caste, creed, gender, class, identity, language, religion, region and so on. In simple terms equality is treating everyone equally with respect and giving equal opportunities. Now to answer the question why do we need equality, in a social context, it becomes evident that it involves the equitable distribution of resources, opportunities, and rights without any form of discrimination. These rights of equality are not merely bestowed by legal systems; rather, they are inherent natural rights. Every individual, regardless of any discriminatory factors, has the right to be treated with dignity, respect, and to access equal opportunities.

To achieve equality in our country which has historically oppressed people based on caste and endured the hardships of colonial rule, it is essential to strive for **equity**—ensuring that everyone has a fair and just opportunity, with fair competition. To accomplish this, a government must guarantee that equality within the nation is a fundamental right. Furthermore, it should recognize that equality is not only a legal entitlement but also an inherent natural right, thus our constitution ensures this in **Part IV Article 14**:

"The state shall not deny to any person equality before law or the equal protection of the laws within the territory of India."

This article consists of two essential components:

1. **Equality before the Law**: This part ensures that everyone is treated equally in the eyes of the law. It implies the absence of any privilege in favour of any person.
2. **Equal Protection of the Laws**: This part mandates that the same law applies to all individuals across society. It expects positive action from the state to ensure fairness.

Through the lights of article 14 we can understand how a state treats its people and ensures one's natural right of equality; however, our history of caste-based oppression and colonial rule has left a significant portion of the population economically disadvantaged and politically and socially marginalized. To truly achieve equality for them, equal treatment alone is insufficient. We require affirmative actions that empower them across all dimensions. Initiatives such as reservations in education and employment opportunities help uplift these marginalized groups, allowing them to attain equal status alongside those who have not faced such adversity. This positive discrimination benefits society as a whole. To achieve this, we must first eliminate discrimination. Simultaneously, affirmative actions should also be implemented.

It is enshrined in our constitution in **Article 15**:

1. *The State shall not discriminate against any citizen on grounds only of religion, race, caste, sex, place of birth or any of them.*

2. *No citizen shall, on grounds only of religion, race, caste, sex, place of birth or any of them, be subject to any disability, liability, restriction or condition with regard to*

(a)access to shops, public restaurants, hotels and places of public entertainment;
(b) the use of wells, tanks, bathing ghats, roads and places of public resort maintained wholly or partly out of State funds or dedicated to the use of the general public.

The clause (1) and (2) of article 15 prohibit discrimination against its citizens on the grounds of caste, religion, sex, race, place of birth, also no citizen shall be subject to any disability, liability, restriction, or condition solely based on the above-mentioned grounds. This applies to:

- **Access to Public Places:** Citizens cannot be discriminated against when accessing shops, public restaurants, hotels, and places of public entertainment.
- **Use of Public Facilities:** Citizens have equal rights to use wells, tanks, bathing ghats, roads, and other public facilities maintained either wholly or partly by the State.

Article 14 and 15, Clauses (1) and (2) focus on ensuring legal equality. However, achieving true equality requires more than just treating everyone the same. It's essential to address the historical oppression faced by marginalized groups based on caste, gender, and other factors. To uplift these marginalized communities, the state may implement measures such as reservation or positive discrimination. For this clause (3) and (4) of article 15, provide power to the parliament to make law for their upliftment. Also, our constitution recognizes education as a fundamental right. It plays a crucial role in shaping both individuals and the nation. Literacy contributes significantly to a country's growth and development across various aspects. Additionally, education is key to uplifting marginalized communities and fostering economic and social progress.

Aiming at this, clause (5) and (6) provides reservation for socially, economically weaker sections in education, the detailed evolution of this is discussed in the next section.

3.Nothing in this article shall prevent the State from making any special provision for women and children.

4.Nothing in this article or in clause (2) of article 29 shall prevent the State from making any special provision for the advancement of any socially and educationally backward classes of citizens or for the Scheduled Castes and the Scheduled Tribes. (1st amendment,1951-special provisions for the advancement of backward classes)

5.Nothing in this article or in sub-clause (g) of clause (1) of article 19 shall prevent the State from making any special provision, by law, for the advancement of any socially and educationally backward classes of citizens or for the Scheduled Castes or the Scheduled Tribes in so far as such special provisions relate to their admission to educational institutions including private educational institutions, whether aided or unaided by the State, other than the minority educational institutions referred to in clause (1) of article 30. (93rd amendment,2006-provision of reservation for Backward, SC, ST classes in private institutions.)

6.Nothing in this article or sub-clause (g) of clause (1) of article 19 or clause (2) of article 29 shall prevent the State from making, —

(a) any special provision for the advancement of any economically weaker sections of citizens other than the classes mentioned in clauses (4) and (5); and

(b) any special provision for the advancement of any economically weaker sections of citizens other than the classes mentioned in clauses (4) and (5) in so far as such special provisions relate to their admission to educational institutions including private educational institutions, whether aided or unaided by the State, other than the minority educational institutions referred to in clause (1) of article 30, which in the case of reservation would be in addition to the existing reservations and subject to a maximum of ten per cent. of the total seats in each category.

In this article clauses (3) to (6) are affirmations to empower the statuses of Women, oppressed classes and economically weaker sections of the society.

- **Special Provisions for Women and Children:** Article 15 does not prevent the State from making special provisions for women and children. These provisions can address their unique needs and challenges.
- **Advancement of Backward Classes and Scheduled Castes/Tribes:** The State can make special provisions for the advancement of socially and educationally backward classes or for the Scheduled Castes and

Scheduled Tribes.

- **Admission to Educational Institutions:** The State can also create special provisions for the advancement of socially and educationally backward classes, Scheduled Castes, and Scheduled Tribes concerning their admission to educational institutions (including private ones).

As we have observed, it is crucial to promote both social and economic equality. Providing equal employment opportunities for marginalized individuals is essential for enhancing their economic status, which, in turn, contributes to social respect. The constitution enshrines some affirmative steps for the marginalized sections of the society in employment in **Article 16:**

(1) There shall be equality of opportunity for all citizens in matters relating to employment or appointment to any office under the State,

(2) No citizen shall, on grounds only of religion, race, caste, sex, descent, place of birth, residence or any of them, be ineligible for, or discriminated against in respect of, any employment or office under the State.

The clauses (1) & (2) of this article aims for the equality of opportunity in employment and prohibition of discrimination in the same.

Equality of Opportunity: Clause (1) ensures that there is equality of opportunity for all citizens in matters related to employment or appointment to any office under the State.

Non-Discrimination: Clause (2) explicitly states that no citizen can be ineligible for, or discriminated against, in respect of any employment or office under the State solely based on the aforementioned grounds.

(3) Nothing in this article shall prevent Parliament from making any law prescribing, in regard to a class or classes of employment or appointment to an office under the Government of, or any local or other authority within, a State or Union territory, any requirement as to residence within that State or Union territory prior to such employment or appointment. (reservation of posts in public employment on the basis of residence)

(4) Nothing in this article shall prevent the State from making any provision for the reservation of appointments or posts in favor of any backward class of citizens which, in the opinion of the State, is not adequately represented in the services under the State. (reservation in public employment for backward classes)

(4A) Nothing in this article shall prevent the State from making any provision for reservation in matters of promotion, with consequential

seniority, to any class or classes of posts in the services under the State in favor of Scheduled Castes and the Scheduled Tribes which in the opinion of State are not adequately represented in the services under the State.

(4B)Nothing in this article shall prevent the State from considering any unfilled vacancies of a year which are reserved for being filled up in that year in accordance with any provision for reservation made under clause (4) or clause (4A) as a separate class of vacancies to be filled up in any succeeding year or years and such class of vacancies shall not be considered together with the vacancies of the year in which they are being filled up for determining the ceiling of fifty per cent, reservation on total number of vacancies of that year.

(5) Nothing in this article shall affect the operation of any law which provides that the incumbent of an office in connection with the affairs of any religious or denominational institution or any member of the governing body thereof shall be a person professing a particular religion or belonging to a particular denomination.

(6) Nothing in this article shall prevent the State from making any provision for the reservation of appointments or posts in favor of any economically weaker sections of citizens other than the classes mentioned in clause (4), in addition to the existing reservation and subject to a maximum of ten per cent. of the posts in each category.

The clauses (3) to (4) of this article affirms employment opportunities for backward class, scheduled class, scheduled tribes and in the promotion of the job.

1. **Reservation for Backward Classes**: The State can make provisions for the reservation of appointments or posts in favor of any backward class of citizens that is not adequately represented in the services under the State. This affirmative action aims to promote equality among different sections of society.

2. **Promotion Reservations for SCs and STs**: Article 16 also allows for reservation in matters of promotion with consequential seniority for Scheduled Castes (SCs) and Scheduled Tribes (STs).

3. **Ceiling on Reservations**: There are provisions for considering unfilled vacancies of a year reserved for being filled up in that year as a separate class of vacancies for succeeding years. This ensures that the total number of reserved vacancies does not exceed fifty percent of the total vacancies in a given year.

4. **Economically Weaker Sections**: Provisions can be made for the reservation of appointments or posts in favor of economically weaker sections of citizens (other than the classes mentioned in clause 4), subject to a maximum of ten percent of the posts in each category.

As previously discussed, our constitution's provisions not only prohibit discrimination but also facilitate oppressed individuals in achieving equal status by promoting educational and employment opportunities. These measures represent affirmative actions taken by the government to attain equality and uplift marginalized people who have faced centuries of oppression. Additionally, the government is committed to promoting equality and eliminating discrimination. The next crucial step our constitutional makers focused on was abolishing the practice of untouchability and eradicating it entirely. **Article 17** is as:

"Untouchability" is abolished and its practice in any form is forbidden. The enforcement of any disability arising out of "Untouchability" shall be an offense punishable in accordance with law.

- Article 17 explicitly states that "Untouchability" is abolished and its practice in any form is forbidden.
- The enforcement of any disability arising out of "Untouchability" is considered an offense punishable in accordance with the law.
- This provision reflects India's commitment to ensuring equal rights and dignity for all citizens

In addition to the fundamental rights mentioned earlier, the other provisions in the constitution for the upliftment of the marginalized communities are:

- **Article 330-342A:** These provisions are related to defining SC, ST, their representations, minority groups and their reservation, establishment of commissions such as NCST, NCSC, NCBC.
- **Article 45: Compulsory** and free education till age 14
- **Article 39A:** Free legal aid

Thus, in order to know about reservation, it becomes crucial to comprehend these constitutional articles, their emphasis, meaning, evolution, and, most importantly, to analyse the significance of these provisions.

CHAPTER SIX

RESERVATION IN INDIA

The term "**reservation**" originates from the Latin word "**reservare**," meaning "to keep back" or "to save." This evolved through Old French as "**reserver**" and into Middle English as "**reservacion.**". In the context of social policy, reservation refers to a system designed to allocate a specific percentage of opportunities—such as jobs, educational seats, and other societal benefits—to underrepresented or disadvantaged groups. The primary aim of this policy is to address historical injustices, social inequality, and systemic discrimination, ensuring these groups have equitable access to opportunities and resources. Halfway across the world, in the vibrant and complex tapestry of India, the caste system had long dictated social hierarchy. The British colonial administration began to introduce reservation policies to address these entrenched inequalities. But it was after India gained independence that reservation truly took shape, enshrined in the Constitution to uplift the Scheduled Castes (SC), Scheduled Tribes (ST), and Other Backward Classes (OBC).

Many countries witnessed social injustice based on colur, class but most of them do not have a reservation policy similar to the one in India. However, they have implemented various **affirmative action** and **equal opportunity** policies to address social inequalities and promote diversity in education and employment. These policies aim to ensure that underrepresented groups have fair access to opportunities, but they do not involve specific quotas or reservations.

6.1 AFFIRMATIVE ACTIONS AND RESERVATION:

While both affirmative action and reservation policies aim to address social inequalities and promote inclusivity, they differ in their approaches and implementations across different regions, particularly in the context of the United States and India. They are commonly used in countries like the United States, Canada, and parts of Europe:

- **Non-Quota-Based**: Affirmative action policies do not typically involve strict quotas. Instead, they focus on creating equal opportunities by considering the background of applicants in admissions, hiring, and promotions.
- **Merit and Diversity**: These policies aim to enhance diversity by giving preference to underrepresented groups when candidates have comparable qualifications.
- **Legal Framework**: Affirmative action is governed by anti-discrimination laws and policies, which ensure fair treatment while aiming to redress historical disadvantages.
- **Focus Areas**: These policies address various forms of inequality, including race, gender, ethnicity, and disability

The key difference between these two policies lay in their approaches. Affirmative action was like a flexible loom, weaving diversity into the fabric of society by considering various factors like race, gender, and ethnicity. It aimed to create a rich tapestry where every thread, regardless of its origin, had a place. In contrast, the reservation system was more rigid, a sturdy frame ensuring specific sections of society were given a predefined percentage of opportunities. It was a necessary rigidity, born out of centuries of caste-based oppression, ensuring that the historically downtrodden could finally rise. In the UK, for example, positive action allowed companies to encourage applications from underrepresented groups without mandating fixed numbers. In India, however, the reservation system explicitly outlined quotas—like 15% for SCs, 7.5% for STs, and 27% for OBCs in government jobs and educational institutions. This clear delineation helped ensure that opportunities reached those who needed them most, but it also sparked debates about meritocracy and the best ways to achieve social justice.

Despite their differences, both affirmative action and reservation shared a unified goal: to mend the rifts created by historical injustices and to weave a society where everyone had a fair chance. Whether it was through the flexible threads of affirmative action or the rigid yet necessary structure of reservation, these policies sought to create a world where the content of one's character mattered more than the circumstances of their birth. And so, in the grand tapestry of social justice, these policies stand as testaments to humanity's enduring quest for equality, each with its own unique pattern, yet both striving to make the world a more inclusive place.

6.2 ORIGIN OF RESERVATION (IN INDIA):

Reservation in India predates colonial rule in India. Let us look into the origin of reservation in India in detail.

As we know the concept of caste has ancient roots in India, dating back over 1,500 years. However, the idea of reservation emerged much later, specifically in the late 19th century. Leaders like **Chatrapathi Shahu of Kolhapur** and the **Mysore Raja KrishnarajaWadiyar** took the pioneering steps towards social justice. Shahu's initiatives in 1902 introduced reservations favouring non-Brahmin and backward classes, along with free education and employment opportunities. Similarly, the 1918 committee in Mysore aimed to counter Brahmin dominance by implementing reservation in government jobs and education. The imperial government in Westminster also played a role, introducing elements of reservation in government of India act 1909.However, it was communal award of 1932 that sparked significant debate. Proposed by **Britishminister Ramsay Macdonald**, it aimed to provide separate representation for various religious and social groups including Muslims, Sikhs, and depressed classes. This proposal was met with resistance with Gandhi fasting in protest. Yet, leader like **B.R. Ambedkar** saw it as a step towards empowering marginalized communities. The eventual agreement known as the Poona Pact, ensured reserved seats for Dalits within a single Hindu electorate, while other religious group retained separate electorates.

In the late 19th century, the seeds of caste-based reservation were planted in India by forward-thinking individuals who recognized the need to address social inequities. Between 1882 and 1891, **William Hunter and Jyoti Rao Phule** proposed the concept of reservation, emphasizing the importance of positive discrimination to uplift marginalized communities. This idea resonated across British India, as voices clamored for systemic changes to bridge the social chasm. In 1902, Maharaja Chatrapati Shahu of Kolhapur took a groundbreaking step by introducing reservations for non-Brahmin and backward classes. Alongside this, he championed free education and employment opportunities, setting a precedent for future affirmative action policies. This initiative was a beacon of hope for many who had long been denied access to these essential resources.

By 1909, the **Government of India Act** had incorporated elements of reservation, acknowledging the necessity of affirmative action within governance. This move was a significant step towards institutionalizing the concept of reservation, providing a framework for its implementation. In **1918, Mysore Raja Nalvadi Krishnaraja Wadiyar** formed a committee to implement reservations for non-Brahmins in government jobs and education, despite facing opposition from Diwan **M. Visvesvaraya**. This effort underscored the growing recognition of the need for equitable opportunities, challenging the entrenched caste hierarchies.

Three years later, in **1921, the Justice Party** government passed the first communal government order legislating reservations. This pioneering move set a legal precedent, formalizing the practice of providing reserved seats and jobs to marginalized communities, thereby laying the groundwork for future policies. The Madras Presidency took a significant step in 1927 by instituting a comprehensive reservation policy: **44% for non-Brahmin Hindus, 16% for Brahmins, Muslims, Christians, and Anglo-Indians, and 8% for Scheduled Castes.** This policy aimed to ensure that diverse social groups were adequately represented in public services and education, acknowledging the multifaceted nature of social disparities.

In 1932, British Prime **Minister Ramsay MacDonald** proposed the Communal Award, which sought to provide separate representation for various religious and social groups, including the depressed classes. This proposal sparked significant controversy and debate. Mahatma Gandhi vehemently opposed the Communal Award, advocating for a unified Hindu electorate instead of separate representations. His protest led to intense negotiations between September and October 1932, culminating in the Poona Pact. This agreement ensured reserved seats for Dalits within a single Hindu electorate, while other religious groups retained separate electorates. The Poona Pact was a landmark moment, balancing the need for representation with the goal of maintaining a unified national identity.

These early efforts and milestones in the history of reservation policies in India laid the foundation for a more inclusive and equitable society. They illustrate a journey of resistance, reform, and negotiation, highlighting the complexities and challenges in addressing social disparities.

TIMELINE

- **1882 and 1891:** *The concept of reservation based on caste was first proposed by William Hunter and Jyoti Rao Phule. Demands for positive discrimination were raised in various parts of British India, highlighting the need to address social disparities.*

- **1902:** *Maharaja Chatrapati Shahu of Kolhapur introduced reservation in favor of non-brahmin and backward classes, along with initiative for free education and employment opportunities.*

- **1909:** *The government of India Act introduces elements of reservation acknowledging the need for affirmative action in governance.*

- **1918:** *Mysore Raja Nalvadi Krishnaraja Wadiyar forms a committee to implement reservations for non-brahmins in government jobs and education, despite opposition from Diwan M.Viswesvaraya.*

- **1921:** *The first Justice Party government passes the first communal government order legislating reservation, setting a precedent for future policies.*

- **1927:** *The Madras presidency provided 44% reservation to non-Brahmin Hindus, 16% to Brahmins, Muslims, Christians, and Anglo-Indians, and 8% to Scheduled Castes.*

- **1932: British** *Prime minister Ramsay MacDonald proposes the Communal Award, aiming to provide separate representation for various religious and social groups, including depressed classes.*
- **1932(September):** Gandhi protests against the communal Award, advocating for a unified Hindu electorate.

- **1932(September-October):** Negotiations *lead to the Poona Pact, ensuring reserved seats for Dalits within a single Hindu electorate,* while other religious groups retained separate electorates.

6.3 POST INDEPENDENCE EVOLUTION:

Following independence, major initiatives were launched in favor of the scheduled caste and scheduled tribes to address the historic discrimination and social justice. The terms scheduled caste and scheduled tribes were recognised by the constitution.

As per *Article 366 (24)* of Constitution of India the Scheduled Castes is defined as:

Such castes, races or tribes or part of or groups within such castes, races or tribes as are deemed under Article 341 to be Scheduled Castes for the purpose of this [Indian] constitution.

As per **Article 366 (25)** of Constitution of India the Scheduled Tribes is defined as:

Such tribes or tribal communities or part of or groups within such tribes or tribal communities as are deemed under Article 342 to the Scheduled Tribes for the purposes of this [Indian] Constitution.

The **Article 341 and 342** of the Indian constitution empowers the **President of India,** to specify scheduled caste and tribes for a particular state or union territory by the following steps:

1. **Consultation:** The President, after consulting with the Governor of the concerned state or union territory, may specify certain castes, races, or tribes as SCs through a public notification.
2. **Recognition Criteria:** The recognition is based on social, educational, and economic backwardness faced by these communities.
3. **Legislative Control:** While the President initiates the process, Parliament has the authority to include or exclude castes, races, or tribes from the list of Scheduled Castes specified in the notification. However, once notified, subsequent changes cannot be made without legislative action.

The complete list of castes and tribes was made via two orders: The Constitution (Scheduled Castes) Order, 1950 and The Constitution (Scheduled Tribes) Order, 1950, respectively. Which are derived from colonial lists and first updated in Scheduled Castes and Scheduled Tribes Lists (Modification) Order, 1956.

Reservations were initially introduced for a period of 10 years and only for SCs and STs, but it kept on extending with several changes in it. This progression of reservation in India aims to uplift every socially and economically disadvantaged group within society

Some of key important evolutions of reservation and its background are:

- **1951:** In the case **state of Madras vs Champakam** which revolved around admission of students in engineering and medical colleges, the supreme court invalidated the reservation for the backward classes.
- **1953:** In response to the judgment, the parliament paved a way for the reservation for the backward classes. It set up **First backward classes commission,** under the chairmanship of social reformer **Kaka Kalelkar** was appointed to determine the criteria for assessing backwardness. The commission submitted its report in March 1955 and considered caste a relevant criterion to determine backwardness It listed 2,399 backward castes or communities, with 837 of them classified as 'most backwards. The report was never implemented.
- In **1954** the Ministry of Education in India suggested that 20% of seats should be reserved for Scheduled Castes (SCs) and Scheduled Tribes (STs) in educational institutions. Additionally, there was a provision to relax minimum qualifying marks for admission by 5% wherever required1. This reservation system aimed to provide historically disadvantaged groups with representation in education and opportunities.
- **1978:** By then president Moraji Desai, the second backward class commission was set up in December 1978 under the chairmanship of former chief minister of Bihar **B.P. Mandel,** to determine the criteria for defining socially economically backward classes. The report was submitted in 1980.By then, the Morarji Desai government had fallen and Indira Gandhi came to power. It remained in deep freeze during her term and that of Rajiv Gandhi.

6.4 MANDEL COMMISSION:

As we step back into Indian history, we encounter a pivotal moment that would go on to reshape the nation's socio-political landscape: the birth of the Mandal Commission. This governmental body, born on January 1, 1979, was charged with a monumental mission—addressing caste-based inequalities through reservation policies. Chaired by B.P. Mandal, the commission was tasked with identifying socially and educationally backward classes. Their objective was to develop comprehensive criteria encompassing social, economic, and educational realms to pinpoint those in dire need of affirmative action.

6.4.1 A Decade of Deliberation

After a decade of exhaustive research and intense deliberation, the Mandal Commission unveiled its findings on December 31, 1980. The report was a treasure trove of insights, highlighting the prevalence of backwardness among a significant portion of India's population. The commission's exhaustive survey and analysis revealed that Other Backward Classes (OBCs) constituted nearly 52% of the population, excluding Scheduled Castes (SCs) and Scheduled Tribes (STs). Their recommendations included a 27% reservation for these communities in educational institutions and public employment.

6.4.2 The Historic Announcement:

Fast forward to 1990, and the echoes of the Mandal Commission reverberated through the halls of Parliament. Prime Minister V.P. Singh's historic announcement to implement the commission's recommendations shook the nation. It was a bold move, aimed at increasing the representation of OBCs in education and government. However, it sparked a wave of protests, particularly from upper-caste communities who felt threatened by the shift in the socio-economic equilibrium.

6.4.3 Contextual Milestones:

To appreciate the full impact of the Mandal Commission, it's essential to consider the broader historical context and various milestones leading up to and following its establishment:

- 1951: The landmark case of State of Madras vs. Champakam Dorairajan, centered around admission to engineering and medical colleges, led the Supreme Court to invalidate reservations for backward classes. This decision underscored the complexities of balancing meritocracy with social justice.

- 1953: In response to the Supreme Court judgment, Parliament established the First Backward Classes Commission under the chairmanship of social reformer Kaka Kalelkar. The commission's 1955 report identified 2,399 backward castes or communities, 837 of which were classified as 'most backward.' However, the report was never implemented, reflecting the contentious nature of the issue.
- 1954: The Ministry of Education recommended that 20% of seats in educational institutions be reserved for SCs and STs, with provisions to relax minimum qualifying marks by 5% where necessary. This policy aimed to enhance representation for historically disadvantaged groups in education.
- 1978: The Second Backward Classes Commission, led by former Bihar Chief Minister B.P. Mandal, was established by then Prime Minister Morarji Desai. This commission was tasked with defining socially and economically backward classes. The commission submitted its report in 1980, but it remained in political limbo during the tenures of Indira Gandhi and Rajiv Gandhi until Prime Minister V.P. Singh's decisive action in 1990.

6.4.5 The Mandal Commission's Impact:

The implementation of the Mandal Commission's recommendations in 1990 had a profound and lasting impact on Indian society. It significantly increased OBC representation in education and government, prompting a broader public discourse on caste discrimination and social justice. Despite the controversy and resistance, the commission's legacy endures, symbolizing a crucial step toward a more inclusive and equitable India.

6.4.6 Post-1980s Timeline:

- **1982: The Foundation is Laid**

The early 1980s marked a significant evolution in reservation policies. It was in this year that the Indian government officially stipulated that 15% and 7.5% of vacancies in the public sector and government-aided institutions should be reserved for Scheduled Castes (SCs) and Scheduled Tribes (STs), respectively. This foundational step was crucial in institutionalizing affirmative action, ensuring guaranteed employment opportunities for these historically marginalized communities.

- **1990:The Mandal Commission Implementation and Its Aftermath**

The dawn of the 1990s brought a seismic shift in India's socio-political landscape. Prime Minister P.V. Narasimha Rao decided to implement the recommendations of the Mandal Commission, which had been set up a decade earlier to address the needs of Other Backward Classes (OBCs). Led by B.P. Mandal, the commission had identified that OBCs constituted nearly 52% of the Indian population and recommended a 27% reservation for them in public employment and educational institutions.

The announcement sparked widespread protests, particularly from upper-caste communities who feared a reduction in their opportunities. The nation witnessed tumultuous scenes as students and professionals took to the streets in dissent. Amidst this chaos, a writ petition was filed in the Supreme Court, leading to the landmark case Indra Sawhney vs. Union of India in 1992.

- **1992: The Landmark Indra Sawhney Judgment:**

The Supreme Court's judgment in the Indra Sawhney case was transformative:

- **Ceiling on Quotas**: The court upheld a ceiling of 50% on total reservations to maintain a balance in opportunities.
- **Social Backwardness Criteria**: The concept of "social backwardness" was emphasized, with the court prescribing 11 indicators to ascertain backwardness.
- **Creamy Layer Concept**: The court introduced the "creamy layer" concept, which excluded the more affluent members of OBCs from reservation benefits. Initially set at an annual income threshold of ₹ 100,000 in 1993, this limit was periodically revised, reaching ₹800,000 by 2015.
- **No Reservation in Promotion**: The court ruled against reservations in promotions within public employment.
- **Permanent Statutory Body**: It recommended the establishment of a permanent statutory body to examine complaints regarding the inclusion or exclusion of communities in reservation lists, leading to the

creation of the National Backward Classes Commission.

- **1995-2000: Constitutional Amendments and the Carry Forward Rule:**

The mid-1990s to early 2000s saw further legislative developments:

- <u>**77th Amendment**</u>: Introduced Article 16(4A), allowing states to provide reservations for SCs and STs in promotions if they were not adequately represented in public employment.
- <u>**81st Amendment**</u>: Added Article 16(4B), permitting the carry forward of unfilled vacancies from previous years, allowing reservation in promotions to exceed the 50% cap set for regular reservations. This became known as the Carry Forward Rule.

- **2019: Broadening Affirmative Action:**

In a significant policy shift, the government announced a 10% reservation in educational institutions and government jobs for economically weaker sections (EWS) from the general category. This policy extended the scope of affirmative action beyond caste-based considerations, recognizing economic disadvantage as a key factor in social justice.

- **2022: The Janhit Abhiyan Case**

In a landmark decision, the Supreme Court, in the case of Janhit Abhiyan vs. Union of India, upheld the validity of the 103rd Constitutional Amendment. This amendment introduced reservations for EWS in educational institutions and government jobs. The court also asserted that the 50% cap on quotas was not inviolable, advocating for affirmative action based on economic grounds. This amendment raised the total reservation to 59.5% in central institutions, marking a significant expansion of the reservation framework.

Reservation Category Percentage
Scheduled Caste 15%
Scheduled Tribe 7.5
Other Backward Class 27%
Economically Weaker Section 10%

TOTAL

59.5%

CHAPTER SEVEN

RESERVATION IN TAMILNADU

As observed thus far, India's reservation system has been multifaceted, addressing needs, origins, existence, evolution, and provisions. It uniquely benefits millions across generations, fostering social, political, and economic upliftment. Among all states and union territories, one stands out: *Tamil Nadu,* which surpasses the 50% reservation limit, While Maharashtra, Karnataka, Gujarat, and Uttar Pradesh grapple with fixing reservation quotas beyond 50%, Tamil Nadu stands out by successfully implementing a 69% reservation. What makes this south state distinctive? What are those exceptional affirmative actions in the state of Tamil Nadu? What were the key developments in Tamil Nadu during both pre-independence and post-independence periods that contributed to its distinctive status? How does this help Tamil people and what was the need? Let us explore and discover answers for these queries.

7.1 EVOLUTION OF CASTE SYSTEM IN TAMIL NADU:

As read in the Origin of Caste, early Tamil has no traces of practicing castes whereas they were divided by the type of land they lived in. During the Sangam era, discrimination based on caste or gender was not widespread despite existing societal hierarchies. Later, in the third century, Brahmins, like other social groups, resided in the Mullai and Marutham tracts. These clusters of Brahmin households were known as parppana-ceri. While we observe the early signs of a caste system within Brahmin communities, the larger Tamil society remained casteless during this period.

However, with the formation of states and the rise of ruling dynasties such as the Pallavas, Pandyas, Cheras, and Cholas, there occurred a significant migration of Brahmins from northern India. These Brahmins brought with them special skills and played a crucial role in shaping Indian culture. Unlike the Vedic Brahmins, who primarily performed yagyas (rituals) for material well-being, the new Brahmins were known for establishing villages. The Brahmins invited by ambitious warlords and kings were instrumental in **establishing temples**, thereby transforming local village gods into forms of mainstream **Puranic gods**. The temple became the **centre for tax collection** and also fostered cultural development in art, music, and literature. The lands received by Brahmins were known as **Brahmadeya land**, and the areas where Brahmins resided were called **Agraharas**.

In this way, the caste in Tamil society uprooted, the rigid caste system in Tamil society manifested through the left-hand (Idangai) and right-hand (Valangai) conflict. The division was rooted in the **clash of interests** between two groups:

- **Right-hand**: Land-owning communities.
- **Left-hand**: Merchant and artisanal classes.

These factions sustained due to the **opposition of the right-hand group** to the left-hand caste people using certain privileges they claimed as theirs. Brahmins often mediate in disputes between these groups. While appearing neutral, they may secretly support the cause of the **left-hand caste groups**. These were prevalent till 19th century and even early decades of 20th century and vanished after independence.

7.2 PRE-INDEPENDENCE:

As noted earlier in the origin of reservation, the pre-independence phase laid the basis for affirmative actions to address the inequality that prevailed. The Madras Presidency, within the British Raj, pioneered the use of reservation to ensure justice for disadvantaged groups. However, complaints arose about Brahmin dominance in the government, where they outnumbered others and held senior positions. The Brahmin hegemony in the administration was owing to their better educational opportunities as a result of their superior position in the caste hierarchy. To counter Brahmin dominance and promote representation of non-Brahmins in government workforce, in **Madras presidency,** leaders such as Dr. **C. Natesa Mudaliar, P. T. Theyagaraya Chetty, and T. M. Nair** established **South Indian Liberal Federation** also known as **Justice Party** in **1916.**

Further in 1921, then chief minister of Madras Presidency, **Akaram Subbaroyalu Reddy** issued a Government Order setting up reservation policies in response to complaints about Brahmin dominance in the administration, but it faced immediate opposition and was put on hold. The **Communal Government Order (G.O.) of 1927** was a significant milestone in Tamil Nadu's social justice movement. Issued by the Justice Party government on September 16, 1921, it aimed to address the dominance of Brahmins in government jobs and educational institutions as data from 1912 showed that Brahmins constituted **55% of Deputy Collectors, 83.3% of Sub-Judges,** and **72.6% of District Munsifs.** The G.O. sought to increase the proportion of posts held by non-Brahmins in the Provincial Services, including the Madras Secretariat. It encompassed Indian Christians, Muslims, and Adi-Dravidas (Scheduled Castes).

This order allocates 44% of all posts to non-brahmin hindus, while brahmins, Muslims, Christians and Anglo Indians receive 16% each and Scheduled Caste receives 8%. Despite criticism for not accurately reflecting population shares, social reformer Periyar E.V. Ramasamy endorses the order as a 'compromise' and accepts it.

Here is a quick time line on evolution of reservation in Tamil Nadu:

1916: C.Natesa Mudaliyar,P.T.Theyagaraya Chetty,T.M.Nair established **South Indian Liberation Federation (Justice Party),**to advocate non-brahmins in government workforce

1921: Chief minister Akaram Subbaroyalu initiates a government order to implement reservation but due to oppositions it was put on hold.

1927: The government order also known as **Communal Government Order** is finally implemented.

RESERVATION BY COMMUNAL G.O 1927

Brahmins 16%

Non-Brahmin Hindus 44%

Scheduled Caste 8%

Muslims 16%

Christians 16%

Anglo-Indians 16%

The order was passed by the Justice Party government in 1927, implemented by Chief Minister **P. Subbaroyan.**

6.3 POST INDEPENDENCE:

Let us now answer the questions that were discussed previously. We know that the Indian government aimed to uplift marginalized communities through affirmative action, including reservations in educational institutions and government jobs. Like, any other policies that has challenges it face, this also faced many challenges, one among them is the landmark case **State of Madras vs Champakam.** As mentioned earlier, the Madras Presidency (present-day Tamil Nadu) had a Government Order (G.O.) from 1927 reserving seats for certain castes in educational institutions. Champakam Dorairajan, who belonged to a forward caste, was denied admission to a medical college even though she had higher marks than some students from reserved categories. The Supreme Court sided with Dorairajan. Their reasoning was that the G.O. violated Article 29(2) of the Constitution, which guarantees that no citizen shall be denied admission to educational institutions based on caste. This judgment created a hurdle for affirmative action policies as they were seen as conflicting with fundamental rights. In response to the court judgment, Periyar spearheaded protests across the state. The Congress party too, voiced support for reservations. Recognizing the need for action, Chief Minister K. Kamaraj reached out to Prime Minister Jawaharlal Nehru. Their collaboration resulted in the amendment of Articles 15 and 16 of the Constitution, allowing states to implement quotas in education and government jobs for disadvantaged communities; the **First Amendment of the Indian Constitution in 1951**, allowed the government to make special provisions for socially and educationally backward classes, thus the **Backward classes** were given **25% reservation**

6.3.1 SATTANATHAN COMMISSION:

In **1969** the DMK government led by **Chief Minister M. Karunanidhi,** established a pivotal commission in Tamil Nadu's history of addressing inequalities: **Sattanathan Commission, named after its chairman A.N. Sattanathan,** its primary objective was to analyse the progress of Backward Classes (BCs) in education, economy, and government employment & to suggest measures for improving the socio-economic conditions of BC communities. The commission identified the lack of progress for BCs despite existing policies, it recommended an increase in reservation quotas for BCs in government jobs and educational institutions. This aimed to create a more level playing field. It introduced the concept of a **"creamy layer"** within BCs. This referred to a segment of BCs who, due to better socio-economic standing, might not require reservation benefits as much as more disadvantaged sections. It recognized a subgroup within BCs facing even greater challenges. The commission proposed a separate category for **Most Backward Classes (MBCs)** with dedicated quotas for their upliftment. Upon this the reservation rate in Tamil Nadu reaches **41%**.

In **1971,** the DMK government under **Chief Minister Karunanidhi** increased reservations for Backward Classes (BCs) from **25% to 31%**, and for Scheduled Castes (SCs) and Scheduled Tribes (STs) from **16% to 18%**. Notably, Karunanidhi established the **nation's first-ever Ministry for the Welfare of Backward Classes** during his DMK rule (1971-1976). These changes brought the state's total reservation quota to 49%. Later, the **AIADMK party headed by M.G. Ramachandran,** decided to implement the **creamy layer** principle based on the recommendations of Sattanathan Commission in 1979. In 1979, Ramachandran set up an **economic criterion of Rs. 9,000 annual income** limits for reservation eligibility & tried to exclude better-off BCs from reservations, but faced opposition.

In **1980,** he reversed his decision of economic criteria after the AIADMK faced a close defeat in the 1980 Indian general election in Tamil Nadu. He further raised the quota for the Backward Classes from 31 percent to 50 percent making the **total reservation to 68%**. The forward castes filed a lawsuit in the Supreme Court opposing this which led to the formation of **Second backward class commission** to investigate the real state of backward classes in Tamil Nadu.

6.3.2 AMBASANKAR COMMISSION:

In **1982,** the **Second Backward Classes Commission,** appointed by the MGR government and led by **J.A. Amba Sankar,** discovered that approximately 11 castes, constituting around 34.8 percent of the backward classes, held 50.7 percent of the jobs in the public service commission, occupied 62.7 percent of seats in professional courses, and received 53.4 percent of scholarships. The Commission estimated that the backward class population was approximately 67 percent and recommended adding 17 forward caste groups to the list while removing 34 caste groups. The government eventually included 29 new caste groups in the list of backward classes but maintained the same 68 percent quota for SCs, STs, and backward classes."

In **1987**, the Vanniyar Sangam, the parent organization of the Pattali Makkal Katchi, organized statewide road blockades, vandalized public property, committed arson in Dalit settlements, and felled trees. They were demanding 20 percent reservations in state government jobs and 2 percent reservations in federal government jobs for the Vanniyar caste. Tragically, 21 Vanniyars lost their lives in police firing during these protests. MG Ramachandran, the then Chief Minister, held a meeting with community leaders, but due to his subsequent illness and untimely death, no decision was made.

In **1989**, following the Vanniyar protests, the DMK government divided the 50 percent BC (Backward Class) quota into 30 percent for Other Backward Classes (OBC) and 20 percent for Most Backward Classes (MBC). The Vanniyars became eligible for reservation under the MBC quota, along with 106 other caste groups.

In **1990**, the DMK government, led by Karunanidhi, implemented a division of reservation for Scheduled Castes (SC) and Scheduled Tribes (ST) in Tamil Nadu. This decision was based on the ruling of the Madras High Court. As a result, a **1%** quota was allocated specifically for **STs**. With this addition, the total reservation rate in Tamil Nadu reached **69 percent**.

Below given the evolution of reservation in Tamil Nadu since independence:

"*1951* "

Backward classes 25%
Scheduled caste & Scheduled Tribes 16%
TOTAL : 41%

"*1971*"

Backward classes 31%
Scheduled Caste & Scheduled Tribes 18%
TOTAL: 49%

"*1980*"

Backward classes 50%
Scheduled caste & Scheduled tribe 18%
TOTAL: 68%

"*1989*"

Other backward classes 30%
Most backward classes 20%
Scheduled caste & Scheduled tribe 18%
TOTAL: 68%

"*1990*"

Other backward classes 30%
Most backward classes 20%
Scheduled Castes 18%
Scheduled Tribes 1%
TOTAL: 69%

Now, answering those questions that were initially asked: Tamil Nadu's reservation policy stands out with its 69% reservation, that was gradually implemented for the welfare of its people. The state contributes in many ways for the strong implementation of the affirmative actions and succeeded it. Here comes another question: The Supreme court ruled that reservation should not exceed 50% but Tamil Nadu has 69% reservation how and what are the legal challenges the state faced? Here are the details:

In **1992**, the Supreme Court ruled that the overall reservations allowed should not exceed 50% as per Article 16(4). Following this decision, the Madras High Court ordered the State to reduce it to 50% starting in the academic year 1994-1995.

In **1993**, the **Tamil Nadu Backward Classes, Scheduled Castes, and Scheduled Tribes Bill, 1993** was passed by the Assembly (Act 45 of 1994). The Bill was sent to the President for approval. J. Jayalalithaa's AIADMK government led a cross-party committee of Tamil Nadu politicians to Delhi to meet with the Central government. She also demanded that the Tamil Nadu government's Act be placed in the **Constitution's Ninth Schedule,** ensuring that it cannot be contested in any court. The President's signature confirmed the 69 percent reservation for Tamil Nadu.

In **1994**, Advocate K. M. Vijayan was viciously assaulted and maimed on his way to New Delhi to file a complaint in the Supreme Court challenging the addition of 69 percent reservation in the 9th Schedule. Later, the 69% Reservation was included in the 9th Schedule in the same year.

Thus, despite many legal challenges, Tamil Nadu remains committed to social justice through its robust reservation system.

Here is a timeline of events:

1951

Backward classes are granted 25% reservation.

1969

The first Backward class commission led by A.N. Sattanathan proposed creation of MBC and suggested creamy layer in reservation.

Reservation rate in TN reached 41%

1971

The DMK government under Karunanidhi, increased reservation for BC to 31%and for SC & ST to 18% establishing a separate ministry for Welfare of Backward Class.

1980

MGR reversed the economic criteria policy and raised the quota for BC to 50%, bringing the total reservation to 68%

1982

The Second backward class commission appointed by MGR, headed by Ambasankar finds disparities in job distribution and recommends adding 29 new caste groups to the list.

1987

The Vanniyar sangam conducts widespread protests seeking reservation for the Vanniyar caste resulting in 21 deaths in police firing.

1989

The government splits BC quota into 30% for OBC & 20% for MBC qualifying Vanniyars for reservation under MBC quota.

1990

The DMK government divides reservation for SC and ST based on the decision of the Madras High Court, raising the total reservation to 69% with the addition of 1% quota for STs.

1992

The Supreme Court rules that overall reservation should not exceed 50%, following this Madras High Court orders the state to reduce reservation to 50%

1993

The Tamil Nadu Backward Class Scheduled Class & Scheduled Tribe Bill 1993, is passed and sent to the President for approval J Jayalalitha's government leads a committee to Delhi demanding that the act be placed in **ninth schedule**; to prevent legal challenges and the President confirms 69% reservation.

Present reservation categories with percentage

RESERVATION CATEGORY %

Backward class 26.5%

Backward Class Muslim 3.5%

Most Backward Class &

denotified communities 20%

Scheduled Caste 15%

Scheduled Caste (Arunthathiyars) 3%

Scheduled Tribe 1%

General 31%

AN OFFER, OR RIGHT

The fight for equality has long been a cornerstone of human civilization. Yet, despite progress, the legacies of historical injustices continue to cast long shadows. In an effort to redress these imbalances, societies have implemented policies like reservation and affirmative action. Until now, we've delved into the caste's origins, its discriminatory effects on society, and how it hinders the nation's growth and democratic ideals. We've also examined reservation system primarily seen in countries like India, setting aside of a specific percentage of seats or positions in education and government for historically disadvantaged groups, often based on caste or tribe. Affirmative action, prevalent in countries like the United States, encompasses a broader range of measures, including preferential treatment in admissions, hiring, and contracting, with the aim of increasing representation of underrepresented minorities.

Affirmative action and reservation both represent attempts to rectify historical injustices and create a more equitable society. Both policies have faced criticism. Concerns have been raised about their impact on meritocracy and the potential for unintended consequences. Critics argue that these policies can sometimes lead to reverse discrimination or create a sense of entitlement among beneficiaries. However, proponents emphasize the importance of these measures in addressing historical inequalities and creating a more just and inclusive society. But are these policies merely government provisions for uplifting marginalized communities, or are they constitutional rights aimed at ensuring equality for all citizens? Are these policies special privileges or essential rights that aim on ensuring equality?

Think of the last time you thought about equality. It might be at home while talking with your parents or fighting with a sibling over a slice of pizza. Maybe it happened in a parking space, while placing an order at a restaurant, or even when paying your bill at the grocery store. In all these everyday moments, equality feels natural – a basic right we all take for granted. If equality is a fundamental & natural right, then what about reservation policies? They aim to achieve the very same thing, so shouldn't they also be considered a basic right?

We are living in a democratic republic country where its people are the real rulers, the core ideology of democracy lies in **Equality and Liberty** of its people. To achieve a society where its people are treated equally, we should understand that practically every individual has different needs, different situations and different capabilities. For justice on a systematic level, a state should focus on fairness, considering individual needs and circumstances. Thus, affirmative action (including reservation) focus on historically disadvantaged people and empower them. Let us discuss it in more detail:

We all inherently understand that equality is a fundamental human right. No one should be denied opportunities simply because of their race, gender, ethnicity, or socioeconomic background. Yet, in practice, achieving true equality proves to be a complex endeavour. Some individuals are born into privilege, with access to quality education, abundant resources, and a supportive social network. They inherit a legacy of advantages that pave the way for success in their careers and personal lives.

However, for many others, this picture is vastly different. Generations of systemic discrimination, poverty, and limited access to education have created significant barriers to upward mobility. These individuals face a constant uphill battle, struggling to overcome the disadvantages they inherited. They may lack the necessary resources, connections, and support systems to compete on an equal footing with those who were born into privilege. Simply proclaiming equality without acknowledging these stark realities is like ignoring the uneven terrain of the race. True progress towards a just society requires a focus on **equity.**

What is Equity? Equity refers to fairness and justice, particularly when it comes to access to resources and opportunities. It goes beyond simply treating everyone the same (equality) and focuses on creating a level playing field that acknowledges past disadvantages. Equity aims to bridge the gaps between historically advantaged and people who faced historical oppression by providing additional support or resources to those who need them most. Equity recognizes that providing everyone with the same opportunities does not necessarily lead to equal outcomes. It necessitates addressing the underlying disparities and providing additional support to those who have been historically disadvantaged. This might involve investing in quality education for underprivileged communities, providing access to affordable healthcare, and implementing policies that combat systemic discrimination.

In essence, equity aims to level the playing field, ensuring that everyone has a fair chance to succeed, regardless of their background. It's about recognizing that true equality can only be achieved when we address the unique challenges faced by different individuals and communities and strive to create a society where everyone has the opportunity to reach their full potential.

A Practice that strives for fairness is **Reservation**, it recognizes that certain groups have been systematically denied opportunities for education, employment, and social mobility for generations. Reservation does not bestow an unfair advantage. It simply **provides a bridge** – a designated quota of seats in educational institutions and government jobs – to help historically disadvantaged groups overcome these hurdles. *It's a chance to level the playing field, not a guarantee of success.* Critics might argue that reservation undermines meritocracy. However, true meritocracy can only exist when everyone has had a fair shot at developing their talents. Reservation allows individuals from disadvantaged backgrounds to access the resources and education needed to showcase their true potential. It allows a wider pool of talent to be recognized and contribute to society.

Ultimately, reservation is a tool for building a more just and equitable society. It allows historically marginalized groups to participate meaningfully in areas where they were previously excluded. By creating a platform for them to compete on a more level playing field, reservation paves the way for true equality of opportunity, where success is based on talent and hard work, not on the accident of birth.

"RESERVATION IS A KEY TO EQUALITY"

The question of whether reservation is a privilege or a right demands a clear answer: reservation is a fundamental right, a cornerstone in the pursuit of societal equality. This principle finds its foundation in the Indian Constitution, which enshrines two crucial aspects of equality: equality before the law and the equal protection of the law.

Achieving true justice necessitates a delicate balance between these principles. While equality before the law ensures that everyone is treated equally by the legal system, the equal protection of the law acknowledges that individuals possess unique circumstances and abilities. This necessitates a nuanced approach that considers the specific needs and challenges faced by historically disadvantaged groups. Ultimately, reservation acts as a crucial safeguard, shielding these marginalized communities from the enduring consequences of past oppression. By providing access to education and creating equal opportunities, reservation empowers individuals and strengthens the foundation of a truly equitable society

CHAPTER NINE

RESERVATION AND US (WE PEOPLE)

Imagine a bustling marketplace, a vibrant hub of activity where people from all walks of life converge. Some arrive with overflowing baskets, brimming with the fruits of their ancestors' – generations of privilege, access to quality education, and a network of support. Others, however, arrive with empty hands, burdened by the weight of historical injustices – centuries of systemic discrimination that have denied them access to opportunities, leaving them struggling to catch up.

This marketplace, a metaphor for our society, vividly illustrates the stark disparities that exist. While some individuals inherit a legacy of advantages, others are forced to navigate a challenging terrain, facing obstacles that seem insurmountable. This isn't simply about inequality; it's about a fundamental lack of fairness, a system that systematically disadvantages certain groups based on their social and economic backgrounds.

Enter reservation policies. Like designating specific seats on a bus for women, these policies aim to create a more level playing field. They acknowledge that simply proclaiming equality is insufficient when some individuals are miles behind the starting line. Reservation policies, particularly those based on caste in India, recognize the historical and ongoing impact of systemic discrimination on certain communities. For centuries, the caste system has perpetuated a rigid hierarchy, confining individuals to their assigned social strata. This has resulted in limited access to education, employment, and even basic human dignity for marginalized communities. Reservation policies, by setting aside a specific percentage of seats in education and government jobs, aim to break down these barriers and provide these communities with a much-needed lifeline.

Critics often argue that reservations perpetuate casteism, but this perspective fails to acknowledge the profound impact these policies have had in empowering individuals and communities. By providing access to education and employment, reservations have enabled individuals to break free from the shackles of their caste, to acquire skills and knowledge, and to contribute meaningfully to society. They have empowered individuals to rise above their circumstances, to challenge the deeply ingrained prejudices of the past, and to build a better future for themselves and their families. It's crucial to understand that reservations are not a permanent solution. They are a temporary measure, a bridge to a more equitable future. As society progresses, as systemic discrimination is dismantled, and as opportunities become more equitable for all, the need for these policies will gradually diminish.

Just as the reserved seats on the bus are not about excluding anyone but about creating a more inclusive and comfortable travel experience for women, caste-based reservations are not about excluding anyone but about creating a more just and equitable society where everyone, regardless of their caste, has an equal opportunity to thrive. They are a recognition of the enduring impact of historical injustices and a commitment to building a society where everyone can reach their full potential.

CHAPTER TEN

DO WE STILL NEED RESERVATION?

India has undoubtedly made strides since independence. Education rates are climbing, the economy is booming, and many enjoy a higher standard of living. Yet, the spectres of caste persist, a relic of a bygone era. While it might seem less overt in urban settings, its insidious influence continues to shape lives, opportunities, and societal structures.

As we've seen, caste discrimination, both overt and subtle, remains a stark reality. It permeates every facet of life, from education and employment to social interactions and political representation. The marginalized castes, historically denied basic rights and opportunities, continue to face systemic barriers. While individual success stories of individuals from marginalized castes are inspiring, they cannot obscure the systemic inequalities that perpetuate the caste system. The progress of a few does not negate the challenges faced by the majority. The deep-rooted prejudices and biases that underpin caste discrimination continue to hinder social mobility and economic advancement. The question of whether reservation is still relevant in today's India is complex and multifaceted. While some argue that it has outlived its purpose, others contend that it remains a necessary tool to level the playing field. As long as caste-based discrimination persists, affirmative action measures may be required to ensure that marginalized groups have a fair chance to succeed.

The seeds of India's reservation system were sown in the crucible of the freedom struggle. Recognizing the deep-rooted injustices of the caste system, the founding fathers of the nation envisioned a society where equality would be the cornerstone. The Constitution, a testament to this vision, enshrined provisions for reservations in education and government jobs for Scheduled Castes (SCs), Scheduled Tribes (STs), and Other Backward Classes (OBCs). This was not merely an act of charity, but a deliberate effort to redress historical wrongs and empower communities that had been systematically marginalized for centuries. The initial conception of reservations was as a temporary measure, a bridge to overcome the deep-rooted social and economic disadvantages faced by these communities. The idea was to provide them with a level playing field, enabling them to compete on an equal footing and break free from the shackles of caste-based discrimination. By ensuring their representation in government and educational institutions, reservations were expected to empower these communities, fostering their economic and social upliftment.

However, the reality soon diverged from the initial plan. Despite significant strides made by some, the persistence of caste-based discrimination and the stark realities of social and economic disparities made it evident that reservations were not a mere temporary expedient. The continued exclusion of marginalized communities from positions of power and influence highlighted the deep-seated nature of the problem. The journey towards true equality has been fraught with challenges. While reservations have undoubtedly opened doors for many, the system itself has become a subject of intense debate. Critics argue that it undermines meritocracy and perpetuates a sense of entitlement. Proponents, on the other hand, emphasize the continued need for affirmative action to address the persistent inequalities that continue to plague our society.

The ideal future, one where reservations are no longer needed, would be a society where meritocracy truly reflects the diverse tapestry of India. A society where every individual, irrespective of their caste, creed, or background, has the chance to reach their full potential and contribute meaningfully to the nation's progress. This would require a multi-pronged approach, encompassing not only reservations but also focus efforts on improving access to quality education, eradicating social prejudices, and creating a truly inclusive society where opportunities are equitably distributed.

CHAPTER ELEVEN

BACKBONES OF RESERVATION

Reservation is not just a policy, it's a response to centuries of systemic oppression and discrimination faced by marginalized communities. Learning about the leaders who fought for these rights helps us understand the historical context and the struggles they endured. These leaders were visionaries who challenged the status quo and fought for a more equitable society. Studying their lives and struggles helps us appreciate the vision and courage it took to bring about social change. Understanding the rationale behind reservation fosters empathy and encourages us to support policies that promote social justice and equality. Learning about the struggles of marginalized communities can help break down prejudices and stereotypes, fostering a more inclusive and tolerant society. The stories of these leaders can inspire future generations to fight for social justice and work towards a more equitable and inclusive society.

By learning about the leaders who brought about reservation, we can gain a deeper understanding of the historical context, appreciate the vision of social justice, and contribute to building a more equitable and inclusive society.

11.1.Dr. B.R. AMBEDKAR:

DR.B.R. Ambedkar played a pivotal role in securing reservations for disadvantaged communities in India. Ambedkar, himself facing caste discrimination, became a powerful voice for the upliftment of Scheduled Castes (SC) and Scheduled Tribes (ST). Here are his key contributions:

- **Public Advocacy**: Ambedkar became a prominent leader of the Dalit movement, organizing protests and advocating for the rights of oppressed castes. He published influential works like "Annihilation of Caste," which critiqued the caste system and demanded reforms.

- **Crucial Figure**: As the Chairman of the Drafting Committee of the Indian Constitution, Ambedkar played a central role in enshrining reservations in the document. He faced opposition from those who feared it might undermine meritocracy.
- **Arguments for Inclusion**: Ambedkar countered with arguments about historical injustices faced by SCs and STs. He emphasized the need for affirmative action to ensure these communities had a fair shot at education and government jobs
- **Social Upliftment**: Reservations, for Ambedkar, were a way to break the cycle of poverty and discrimination. He believed increased access to education and employment would empower these communities.
- **Political Representation**: He also saw reservations in legislatures as crucial. By giving these communities a voice in government, they could advocate for their rights and participate in policy decisions.
- **Temporary Measure**: Contrary to a common misconception, Ambedkar envisioned reservations as a temporary measure. His ultimate aim was to dismantle the caste system altogether and create a truly equal society.
- **Education as Key**: Ambedkar believed that education was the cornerstone of progress for marginalized communities. He championed initiatives for increased access to education for SCs and STs.
- **Emphasis on Dignity**: His fight went beyond reservations. He stressed the importance of restoring dignity and challenging social practices that perpetuated caste discrimination.

11.2. JYOTIRAO PHULE:

Jyotirao Phule, a social reformer from the 19th century, is considered a pioneer in advocating for affirmative action policies in India, although the term "reservation" wasn't used at the time.

Precursor to Reservations: While not directly advocating for quotas in government jobs or education, Phule's work laid the groundwork for affirmative action policies. He vehemently opposed the caste system and fought for the upliftment of marginalized communities.

Focus on Education: Phule believed education was crucial for empowering lower castes. He established schools for girls and Shudras (untouchables and other backward castes) to challenge the educational monopolyof upper castes.

Satyashodhak Samaj: In 1873, Phule founded the Satyashodhak Samaj (Society of Seekers of Truth). This social reform organization aimed to dismantle the caste system and promote social justice.

Attacking Brahminical Supremacy: Phule criticized the dominance of Brahmins in society and religious texts. He believed this had led to the subjugation of lower castes.

Paving the Way: Phule's ideas on social justice and uplifting marginalized communities influenced later generations of reformers, including Dr. B.R. Ambedkar, who directly championed reservations in the Constituent Assembly.

While Jyothirao Phule is not credited with directly advocating for reservations in the modern sense, his work on social reform and fighting for the rights of lower castes laid the groundwork for affirmative action policies in India.

11.3. PERIYAR.E.V. RAMASAMY:

Erode Venkata Ramasamy, more popularly known as Periyar or Thanthai Periyar (respected father), was a prominent Indian social reformer and politician from the early 20th century.

Fought Against Caste System: Periyar vehemently opposed the caste system and its associated inequalities. He challenged social norms and campaigned for the upliftment of marginalized communities, particularly the Shudras (untouchables and other backward castes).

Women's Rights Advocate: Periyar advocated for women's rights and criticized patriarchal practices. He championed education for girls and fought against social evils like child marriage.

Initial Support: During his early political career as part of the Indian National Congress, Periyar supported reservation for non-Brahmin communities in government jobs and education. He saw it as a way to address caste-based discrimination and ensure equal opportunities.

Fight Within Congress: In 1922, as President of the Madras Presidency Congress Committee, Periyar strongly advocated for reservations within the party. However, he faced resistance from dominant caste groups.

Disillusionment with Congress: Disappointed by the lack of progress within Congress on issues of caste and social justice, Periyar left the party in 1925. This marked a shift in his stance on reservations.

Focus on Annihilation of Caste: Periyar formed the Self-Respect Movement and the Dravidar Kazhagam. He emphasized the complete eradication of the caste system as the ultimate goal. He believed reservations might create a separate identity for backward castes, perpetuating the caste structure.

Reservation System: Periyar's views on reservation for backward castes are complex. He initially supported it but later advocated for its abolition, favoring a system based on proportional representation. This remains a point of debate.

Dravidian Politics: The Dravidian political parties (DMK, AIADMK) that trace their roots to Periyar have historically supported reservations for backward castes in Tamil Nadu.

11.4. ANNADURAI:

Conjeevaram Natarajan Annadurai, founder of the Dravida Munnetra Kazhagam (DMK) party, was a key figure in promoting the reservation policyin Tamil Nadu.

Political Advocacy: Annadurai's political agenda included strong support for the backward classes, ensuring they had better access to education and employment through reservation policies.

Cultural Reforms: He also advocated for Tamil identity and language, linking cultural pride with social justice initiatives.

11.5. M. KARUNANIDHI:

Muthuvel Karunanidhi, a significant leader of the DMK and a former Chief Minister of Tamil Nadu, expanded and strengthened reservation policies in the state.

Policy Expansion: Karunanidhi's tenure saw the expansion of reservations in educational institutions and government jobs, cementing Tamil Nadu's position as a state with one of the most comprehensive affirmative action programs in India.

Social Welfare: His government also introduced numerous welfare schemes aimed at uplifting the socio-economically backward sections of society.

11.6. K. KAMARAJAR:

Kumaraswami Kamaraj, a prominent Congress leader and former Chief Minister of Tamil Nadu, played a critical role in implementing educational reforms that benefited the backward classes.

Educational Reforms: Kamaraj's tenure is noted for the introduction of the midday meal scheme in schools, which significantly increased school enrolment and attendance among children from poorer backgrounds.

Political Vision: His efforts were geared towards creating an equitable society where education served as a primary tool for social mobility.

11.7. M.G. RAMACHANDRAN (MGR):

Maruthur Gopalan Ramachandran, widely known as MGR, founded the **All-India Anna Dravida Munnetra Kazhagam (AIADMK) and served as Chief Minister of Tamil Nadu.** He played a pivotal role in continuing and expanding the reservation policies aimed at social upliftment.

Policy Continuation and Expansion: MGR's government ensured that the existing reservation policies were effectively implemented and even expanded to include more benefits for the backward classes. This included increasing the reservation quotas in educational institutions and government jobs.

Social Welfare Programs: He introduced several welfare schemes that indirectly supported the backward classes, such as the free midday meal scheme, free school uniforms, and textbooks, which significantly improved educational access and retention rates among economically disadvantaged students.

11.8. JAYALALITHA:

J. Jayalalitha, the former Chief Minister of Tamil Nadu, made significant contributions to the state's reservation policy.

- Under Jayalalithaa's leadership, Tamil Nadu successfully broke the 50% reservation quota set by the Supreme Court.
- The reservation policy across the country typically stands at 50%, but in Tamil Nadu, she increased it to **69%.**
- In the 1990s, the Supreme Court ruled that reservation should not exceed 50%.
- The Madras High Court also directed Tamil Nadu to revise its reservation quota.
- However, Jayalalithaa ensured that the **Tamil Nadu Act of 1994** was passed, providing constitutional protection for the increased reservation.
- The Act included reservation of seats in education and employment for backward classes, scheduled castes, and tribe.
- Jayalalithaa's meetings with then-Prime Minister Narasimha Rao in Delhi were successful.
- She ensured that the Tamil Nadu Act was added to the **Ninth Schedule,** making it immune to legal challenges.
- The Act also addressed the concept of the **"creamy layer,"** which excludes wealthier and educated individuals from government-

sponsored benefits.

11.9 JUSTICE PARTY:

It is notable that the Justice Party of India was the pioneer of reservation that successfully implemented reservation in Madras presidency in 1927.

Pioneers of Reservation Policies: The Justice Party was the first to implement reservations in government jobs and educational institutions for non-Brahmin communities in 1921, setting a precedent for future reservation policies across India.

Educational and Social Reforms: The party established numerous educational institutions to improve access for underprivileged communities and introduced administrative reforms to ensure equitable distribution of resources, challenging traditional caste hierarchies.

Influence on Subsequent Movements: The Justice Party's ideology significantly influenced the Dravidian movement, which continued their legacy of promoting social justice and reservations, impacting the broader Indian social and political landscape

CHAPTER TWELVE

KEY TO EQUALITY

In the bustling tapestry of today's world, opportunities don't always dance evenly across the landscape. Some find themselves standing on a level ground, while others face a steep uphill climb. Reservation policies, like a guiding hand, attempt to mend this uneven terrain. They act as a bridge, connecting underprivileged communities to the avenues of education, employment, and a better life. Reservation is not about handouts, but about hand-ups. It empowers individuals, giving them the tools and opportunities to build a better life for themselves and their families. It's a story of breaking down barriers, of leveling the playing field, and of ensuring that every individual, regardless of their background, has a fair chance to thrive.

- **Development: Building a Strong Foundation**

Imagine a village nestled amidst rolling hills, where generations have toiled the land, yet their dreams of a brighter future often remain distant. Many families struggle to escape the clutches of poverty, their hopes fading with each passing day. Reservation policies, like a lifeline, offer a helping hand. By ensuring a fair share of government and public sector jobs, they provide a stable income, a beacon of hope in the face of hardship. This financial security empowers families to break free from the cycle of poverty, allowing them to invest in their children's education, improve their living conditions, and build a stronger future for themselves and their communities.

- **Education: Unlocking Opportunities**

In every village and every town, children dream big. They dream of becoming doctors, teachers, engineers, and artists. But for many, these dreams remain just that – dreams. Limited access to quality education can be a formidable barrier, hindering their potential. Reservation policies, like a bridge connecting to a brighter future, ensure that students from underprivileged backgrounds have the opportunity to attend schools and universities. They open doors to classrooms, laboratories, and libraries, equipping them with the knowledge and skills necessary to chase their ambitions. By leveling the playing field, these policies unlock the potential of countless individuals, allowing them to contribute meaningfully to society.

- **Job Opportunities: Securing a Bright Future**

The journey from student to professional can be daunting, especially for those who face systemic barriers. Reservation policies, like a guiding light, illuminate the path to a successful career. By reserving a portion of jobs in government and public sectors, they offer a fair chance to individuals from underrepresented communities. These opportunities provide a stable income, a sense of security, and the chance for professional growth. Moreover, some private sector companies have also embraced similar practices, further expanding the horizon of possibilities for those who have been historically marginalized.

- **Living: Improving Quality of Life**

Beyond the realm of education and employment, reservation policies have a profound impact on the overall well-being of marginalized communities. A stable income translates into improved access to essential services like healthcare, quality housing, and nutritious food. It empowers families to live with dignity, free from the constant worry of financial insecurity. Furthermore, by ensuring representation in government and decision-making bodies, reservation policies amplify the voices of the marginalized. Their concerns are heard, their needs are addressed, and policies are formulated with greater inclusivity and fairness.

- **Creating an Inclusive Society:**

Reservation is about more than just providing opportunities; it's about creating a society where everyone has the chance to succeed. By addressing past injustices and ensuring equal opportunities, reservation policies help build a fairer and more inclusive society.

CHAPTER THIRTEEN

ABOLITION AND ANNIHILATION OF CASTE

The concept of "**Annihilation of Caste**" was introduced by **Dr. B.R. Ambedkar** in his **1936** essay of the same name. He argued for the complete dismantling of the caste system, not just its legal abolition, but also its social and psychological aspects. Abolishing caste refers to the removal of legal, social, and economic barriers based on caste identity. It aims to create a society where everyone has equal rights and opportunities regardless of their caste background. Annihilation of caste, a more radical concept, goes beyond abolition and calls for the complete dismantling of the caste system, including its social and psychological aspects. It seeks to create a society free from any trace of caste-based discrimination and hierarchy.

13.1 LEGAL DIMENSION- ABOLITION OF CASTE:

India's journey towards a just and equitable society began with its Constitution, a document born of hope and a commitment to equality. This landmark document, adopted in 1950, enshrined several provisions aimed at dismantling the age-old scourge of caste discrimination.

Article 15, a cornerstone of this constitutional edifice, declared that no citizen shall be discriminated against on the grounds of religion, race, caste, sex, or place of birth. This powerful statement aimed to break down the walls of social exclusion and create a level playing field for all.

Furthermore, **Article 17,** a bold proclamation of social justice, abolished "untouchability" in all its forms. This abhorrent practice, a blot on the nation's conscience, was declared illegal, marking a significant step towards a more humane and inclusive society.

Recognizing the deep-rooted impact of caste-based discrimination, the Constitution also included **Article 46,** which directed the state to promote the educational and economic interests of Scheduled Castes, Scheduled Tribes, and other weaker sections of society. This provision emphasized the need for affirmative action to address historical inequalities and empower marginalized communities.

To further strengthen the fight against caste-based atrocities, the **Scheduled Castes and the Scheduled Tribes (Prevention of Atrocities) Act, 1989,** was enacted. This landmark legislation provided for stringent punishments for acts of violence and discrimination against these communities, sending a strong message that such acts would not be tolerated.

While these legal measures represent a significant step forward, the journey towards a truly caste-free society remains fraught with challenges. Deep-seated prejudices and societal resistance continue to hinder the effective implementation and enforcement of these laws. Despite these hurdles, the Constitution, with its unwavering commitment to equality and justice, remains a beacon of hope. It serves as a constant reminder of the ideals that India strives for, a society where caste no longer defines an individual's destiny, and where everyone enjoys equal rights and opportunities.

13.2. THE SOCIAL DIMENSION: ANNIHILATION OF CASTE:

While the Constitution provides a strong legal framework for caste abolition, it is crucial to recognize that laws alone cannot dismantle a system deeply ingrained in the fabric of society. True change requires a multifaceted approach, one that addresses the deep-rooted social and economic factors that perpetuate caste discrimination.

Education, like a fertile seed, holds the key to cultivating a more inclusive society. By infusing our classrooms with a curriculum that celebrates diversity, champions human rights, and confronts the harsh realities of caste history, we can empower future generations with the knowledge and understanding to dismantle these harmful barriers. Awareness campaigns, like a gentle breeze, can spread the seeds of change. By sharing inspiring stories of individuals who have overcome the shackles of caste and achieved success, these campaigns can challenge deeply held prejudices and inspire hope for a more equitable future.

Economic disparity often exacerbates the divisions created by caste. It's like a quicksand, pulling individuals and communities deeper into poverty and despair. Addressing this requires a concerted effort to ensure equitable access to economic resources. Initiatives like reservations in education and employment, while facing their own set of challenges, aim to level the playing field, providing marginalized communities with the opportunities they deserve. Furthermore, nurturing entrepreneurship and empowering individuals with relevant skills can foster economic independence and break the cycle of poverty, allowing these communities to thrive on their own terms.

Inter-caste marriages, like bridges spanning divides, can play a pivotal role in dismantling the rigid structures of the caste system. These unions, a testament to love and acceptance, challenge deeply ingrained social norms and foster a sense of unity and belonging. By breaking down the walls of prejudice, they pave the way for a more inclusive and harmonious society. Governments and non-profit organizations can act as catalysts for this social transformation. Awareness programs can shed light on the benefits of inter-caste marriages, dispelling myths and fostering understanding. Counselling services can provide support and guidance to couples navigating the complexities of such unions, while legal frameworks can offer protection against societal backlash and ensure their rights are upheld.

Furthermore, ensuring adequate political representation for marginalized communities is crucial for their empowerment and well-being. When the voices of Scheduled Castes and Scheduled Tribes are amplified in legislative bodies, their concerns are more likely to be heard and addressed. This representation ensures that policies and laws are formulated with their needs and aspirations in mind, leading to more equitable and inclusive governance. These initiatives, while not a panacea, are crucial steps towards building a truly casteless society. They symbolize a commitment to social justice and a belief in the transformative power of love, understanding, and equality.

13.3 CHALLENGES:

Despite the strides made in combating caste discrimination, the journey towards a truly casteless society is far from over. The shadows of prejudice still linger, casting a long shadow over our nation.

Deep-rooted prejudices, like stubborn weeds, have taken hold in the very fabric of our society, passed down through generations. These ingrained biases, often unconscious, continue to fuel discrimination and inequality. Changing these deeply held beliefs requires a sustained and concerted effort, a delicate process of nurturing understanding and fostering empathy. Social resistance to change can be a formidable obstacle, particularly in rural communities where traditional norms and hierarchies hold sway. Community leaders, respected elders, and influential figures play a critical role in driving change.

Their voices can act as a powerful catalyst, challenging entrenched beliefs and inspiring others to embrace a more inclusive vision for the future.

Economic disparities, like gaping chasms, further widen the divide between castes. Persistent efforts in education, job creation, and equitable economic policies are crucial to bridge these gaps. Ensuring that everyone has access to opportunities, regardless of their caste background, is essential for breaking the cycle of poverty and empowering marginalized communities.

Furthermore, the gap between legislation and its actual implementation remains a significant challenge. The wheels of justice can grind slowly, and the protection afforded by laws often remains elusive for those who need it most. Strengthening the judicial and law enforcement mechanisms is paramount to ensure that the rights of marginalized communities are upheld and that those who perpetrate acts of discrimination are held accountable.

The abolition and annihilation of caste is not merely a legal obligation; it is a moral imperative, a testament to our commitment to justice and equality. It demands a collective effort, a symphony of voices from all corners of society – the government, civil society organizations, educational institutions, and every individual. By embracing equality as a guiding principle, fostering social justice, and dismantling the entrenched walls of prejudice, we can pave the way for a truly inclusive and equitable society where everyone, regardless of their caste, enjoys equal dignity, respect, and opportunities.

As Dr. B.R. Ambedkar, a visionary who dedicated his life to eradicating caste, profoundly observed, "**Caste is a notion; it is a state of the mind.**" This profound insight underscores the importance of addressing the deep-seated psychological and social aspects of caste. By challenging these deeply ingrained notions, we can begin to dismantle the very foundations of this pernicious system, paving the way for a society where everyone is truly equal, not just in the eyes of the law, but in the everyday realities of life

CHAPTER FOURTEEN

EWS

In the ongoing discourse on reservations in India, the **Economic Weaker Section (EWS) quota** has emerged as a contentious issue, sparking heated debates and raising serious concerns. Unlike other reservation policies, which primarily focus on uplifting historically marginalized communities like **Scheduled Castes (SC), Scheduled Tribes (ST), and Other Backward Classes (OBC),** the EWS quota, introduced in 2019, aims to assist economically disadvantaged individuals from the so-called "**general**" category.

On the surface, this initiative appears to be a step towards greater economic inclusivity, promising to address the needs of those facing financial hardship regardless of their caste or community. The EWS quota, which provides a **10% reservation** in government jobs and educational institutions, targets individuals from the general category whose family income falls below ₹**8 lakhs per annum.** However, a deeper dive into this policy reveals several problematic aspects that cast a shadow over its intent and fairness.

14.1 IS EWS-INJUST?

The EWS reservation, despite its intent to address economic disparity, suffers from several fundamental flaws that undermine its purpose and raise serious concerns about its fairness.

Firstly, the income ceiling of ₹8 lakhs per annum for EWS categorization is excessively high. In a country where a significant portion of the population grapples with poverty and limited access to basic necessities, defining a family earning ₹8 lakhs annually as "**economically weaker**" stretches the definition beyond recognition. This arbitrary threshold fails to accurately reflect the true extent of economic hardship faced by millions of Indians.

Secondly, there's a strong argument that the EWS quota primarily benefits the already privileged sections of society, particularly upper-caste groups. Critics contend that this reservation serves as a strategic move to safeguard the interests of those who have historically enjoyed socio-economic advantages.

By creating a separate category for individuals from the "general" category, the EWS quota dilutes the very essence of affirmative action, which aims to uplift historically marginalized and disadvantaged communities.

Furthermore, the EWS criteria fail to adequately address the genuine economic hardships faced by a large segment of the Indian population. Families earning significantly less than the ₹8 lakh threshold often struggle with basic needs, limited access to quality education, and inadequate healthcare. The EWS criteria, with its high-income ceiling, overlook these critical realities, leaving genuinely impoverished families without the necessary support and opportunities.

14.2 EWS RESERVATION: A HINDERANCE TO SOCIAL JUSTICEAND EQUALITY:

The EWS reservation, despite its intentions, poses a significant threat to the core principles of social justice. Reservations in India have historically served as a crucial tool to address the deep-rooted social and economic inequalities faced by marginalized communities, offering them a pathway to education, employment, and a better future. However, the EWS quota, by prioritizing economic criteria over historical injustices, fundamentally undermines this objective.

Instead of focusing on rectifying the systemic disadvantages faced by Scheduled Castes, Scheduled Tribes, and Other Backward Classes, the EWS quota shifts the focus towards providing benefits to individuals who are already relatively privileged within the "general" category. This shift in focus dilutes the very essence of affirmative action, transforming it from a tool for social justice into a mechanism for providing economic benefits to a section of the population that does not necessarily require such assistance. Furthermore, the EWS reservation, rather than fostering inclusivity, inadvertently creates new inequities. By reserving 10% of seats and jobs for individuals who are economically better off within the general category, it reduces the opportunities available for those who truly need these affirmative action measures. This not only perpetuates existing social inequalities but also breeds a sense of injustice among other reservation categories who continue to face systemic discrimination and lack of access to resources.

Perhaps most significantly, policies like the EWS reservation erode public trust in the very foundation of affirmative action. When reservations are perceived as being manipulated to benefit certain privileged groups, it undermines public faith in the fairness and efficacy of these crucial measures. This erosion of trust can have far-reaching consequences, fueling social unrest, increasing divisions among different social groups, and ultimately hindering the efforts to achieve a truly equitable and just society.

14.3 THE EWS QUOTA: UNINTENDED CONSEQUENCES:

The implementation of the EWS reservation carries with it a set of long-term dangers that threaten to undermine the very foundations of social justice and equality.

Firstly, the EWS quota poses a significant threat to the core principles of affirmative action. By introducing a quota that primarily benefits economically better-off individuals from the "general" category, it dilutes the impact of reservations intended for genuinely marginalized communities like Scheduled Castes, Scheduled Tribes, and Other Backward Classes. This shift in focus, from addressing historical injustices and social inequities to providing benefits to a relatively privileged segment of society, undermines the very essence of affirmative action.

Secondly, the EWS reservation exacerbates the ongoing debate surrounding the impact of reservations on meritocracy. While reservations are often criticized for potentially compromising merit, the EWS quota further amplifies this concern. By extending benefits to individuals who are not the most disadvantaged, it skews the competitive landscape, allowing those who are already relatively well-off to gain an unfair advantage. This not only undermines the principles of fair competition but also fuels resentment and discontent among other sections of society.

Perhaps most alarmingly, the EWS reservation, instead of addressing the root causes of economic inequality, inadvertently perpetuates it. By providing undue advantages to upper-caste groups under the guise of economic assistance, it deepens existing social divides and fosters resentment among genuinely marginalized communities. This can lead to increased social tensions, eroding social cohesion, and hindering the progress towards a truly inclusive and equitable society

71

CHAPTER FIFTEEN

CASTE PRIDE Vs CASTE IDENTITY

In recent years, the discourse surrounding reservations and the role of community certificates in India has been fraught with controversy and misconceptions. Critics often argue that these certificates foster an undue sense of entitlement, implying that the progress of marginalized communities is solely attributable to these documents. They paint a picture where individuals from these communities simply "cash in" on their caste identity, overlooking the years of systemic discrimination, historical disadvantage, and the relentless struggle for social and economic mobility.

However, the reality is far more nuanced. Community certificates are merely a tool, a symbolic recognition of historical injustices and a means to address the deep-rooted inequalities that have plagued these communities for centuries. These certificates, in essence, represent a form of affirmative action, an attempt to level the playing field and provide marginalized communities with a fair chance to compete and succeed. The true enabler of growth, however, lies not in the possession of a certificate, but in a fundamental shift in societal attitudes. It lies in moving away from a culture of caste pride, where one's identity is inextricably linked to their caste, towards a society that embraces inclusivity, celebrates diversity, and recognizes the inherent dignity and worth of every individual, regardless of their background.

For centuries, caste pride has cast a long shadow over Indian society, a venomous weed choking the roots of equality. It thrived on the notion of inherent superiority based solely on birth, a twisted logic that elevated some while systematically oppressing others. Those born into the higher echelons of the caste system, intoxicated by the intoxicating brew of privilege, wielded their power to maintain the status quo. They erected invisible barriers, denying marginalized communities access to education, employment, and even basic human dignity. This insidious caste pride fostered an environment where merit was overshadowed by birthright, where talent was stifled, and where the dreams of countless individuals were crushed under the weight of centuries of injustice.

Community certificates were born out of a deep-seated need to address the centuries-old injustices faced by marginalized communities. They are not a silver bullet, a free pass to success. Instead, they represent a symbolic acknowledgment of the systemic barriers that have historically held these communities back. These barriers, erected by the insidious caste system, have denied generations access to quality education and decent employment opportunities.

Think of community certificates as a bridge, connecting marginalized communities to avenues of opportunity that were once denied to them. They provide a level playing field, ensuring that individuals from these communities have a fair chance to compete and showcase their talents, unburdened by the weight of historical disadvantage. It's crucial to understand that community certificates do not guarantee success. They simply offer a pathway, an opportunity to break free from the shackles of poverty and exclusion. The ultimate goal is to empower individuals through education and employment, enabling them to build a better future for themselves and their families.

Community Certificates: A Tool, Not an Identity

Often, community certificates become synonymous with caste identity, leading to a dangerous conflation of the two. While these certificates often correspond to a particular caste, they should not define an individual's entire being. At their core, they serve as a crucial document, a proof of belonging to a community that has historically faced systemic discrimination and marginalization. This proof allows individuals to access educational opportunities and affirmative action programs designed to level the playing field and provide a fair chance for those who have been historically disadvantaged.

True Pride Lies in Merit, Not Birth:

The notion of caste pride based solely on possessing a community certificate is deeply misplaced. True pride should stem from our achievements, our character, and our contributions to society. Elevating oneself based on the caste one is born into is not pride, but a reflection of a deeply flawed system. Oppressing others or deriving a sense of superiority from their disadvantage is not pride, it is injustice.

Addressing Abuse, Not Abolition:

While there may be instances of misuse or abuse of the reservation system, it's crucial to remember its fundamental purpose: to address historical injustices and provide a level playing field for marginalized communities. The focus should be on strengthening the system, ensuring its fair and equitable implementation, and plugging any loopholes that may be exploited. Abolishing the system entirely would be a grave injustice, effectively denying generations of marginalized individuals the opportunity to overcome the systemic barriers they continue to face.

Education: The True Catalyst for Change

At the heart of community certificates lies the profound understanding that education is the true equalizer. It's a key that unlocks doors to new worlds of knowledge, skills, and opportunities. For generations, systemic barriers erected by the caste system had denied marginalized communities access to quality education, trapping them in cycles of poverty and disadvantage. Community certificates, in this context, act as a bridge, providing access to educational institutions and opening doors that were once firmly shut.

It's crucial to remember that these certificates are not a magic wand. They do not guarantee success. True success stems from the individual's dedication, perseverance, and hard work. We must shift the narrative away from celebrating individuals merely for possessing a certificate and towards celebrating their achievements – their intellectual prowess, their unwavering determination, and their contributions to society. These are the true markers of success, not the label of their origin. By focusing on individual merit and celebrating the power of education to transform lives, we can truly empower marginalized communities and build a more equitable and inclusive society.

The "Casteless Certificate":

The concept of a "casteless certificate" is a fascinating one, though it may not have a formal legal existence. It embodies a powerful aspiration: a society where caste no longer defines an individual's identity or opportunities. Imagine a world where individuals are not pigeonholed by their birth caste. A "casteless certificate" would symbolize a conscious choice to transcend these rigid societal boundaries, to embrace a sense of belonging to humanity as a whole. It would be a declaration of individuality, a rejection of the limitations imposed by a system rooted in historical injustice.

However, this seemingly utopian idea presents significant challenges. In a country where caste-based reservations exist in education, employment, and even political representation, opting for a "casteless certificate" would inevitably limit access to these opportunities designed to address historical inequities. Furthermore, caste often plays a significant role in shaping an individual's social identity. It provides a sense of belonging, a connection to community. Rejecting this aspect of one's identity could lead to a sense of disconnection, a feeling of being adrift from one's roots.

Finally, the practical implementation of such a certificate would require significant legal and administrative reforms. Currently, caste information is often included in official documents like birth certificates. Introducing a "casteless certificate" would necessitate a fundamental shift in how identity is recorded and recognized by the state.

The concept of a "casteless certificate" is a powerful symbol of the aspiration for a truly casteless society. While it may not be a practical solution in its current form, it serves as a reminder of the need to challenge the deeply ingrained structures of caste and strive for a society where individuals are judged solely on their merits and not on the basis of their birth.

The Illusion of a "Casteless" Solution

The concept of a "casteless certificate" might seem like a progressive step towards a caste-free society. However, while it represents a desire to transcend caste boundaries, it's crucial to recognize that simply opting out of a caste designation doesn't automatically dismantle the system.

Just as community certificates, while necessary tools for addressing historical injustices, don't inherently eradicate caste, a **"casteless certificate"** might inadvertently perpetuate the very system it seeks to escape. It focuses on individual detachment from a specific caste rather than promoting a broader understanding of caste as a social construct that needs to be dismantled. This approach may inadvertently reinforce the idea that caste is an individual choice rather than a deeply ingrained social and political reality.

The true enemy in this struggle is not the certificate itself, but the insidious caste pride that seeks to maintain and perpetuate existing hierarchies. It's the belief in inherent superiority based on birth, the resistance to sharing power, and the reluctance to acknowledge and address the historical injustices faced by marginalized communities.

The path towards a truly casteless society lies not in individualistic solutions like "casteless certificates," but in a collective effort to dismantle the structures that perpetuate caste discrimination. This requires a multifaceted approach that includes:

- **Promoting inclusive education:** Fostering a deeper understanding of caste as a social construct and its historical impact.
- **Championing equitable opportunities:** Ensuring equal access to education, employment, and resources for all, regardless of their

background.

- **Combating caste-based discrimination:** Actively challenging and dismantling discriminatory practices in all spheres of life.
- **Building a more inclusive society:** Fostering a culture of respect, empathy, and understanding among all communities.

Ultimately, a "casteless certificate" might be a symbolic gesture, but true change will only come about through a collective effort to dismantle the structures of caste and build a society where everyone, regardless of their origin, has an equal opportunity to thrive.

CHAPTER SIXTEEN

LANDMARK JUDGEMENTS

The Indian judicial system has played a pivotal role in shaping the contours of reservation policies, navigating the delicate balance between equality and affirmative action. Several landmark judgments have not only upheld the constitutional validity of reservations but also refined their scope and implementation.

1. State of Madras vs Champakam Dorairajan, AIR 1951, SC 226
2. M.R. Balaji vs State of Mysore AIR1963 SC 649
3. T. Devadasan vs Union of India,1964 SC 179
4. R. Chitralekha vs State of Mysore AIR 1964 SC 1823
5. P. Rajendran vs State of Madras AIR 1968 SC1012
6. State of Andhra Pradesh vs P. Sagar AIR 1968
7. A. Periya Karuppan vs State of Tamil Nadu AIR 1971 SC2303
8. U.S.V. Balram vs State of Andhra Pradesh AIR 1972 SC1375
9. Kumari K.S. Jayasree vs State of Kerala AIR 1976 SC2318
10. State of Kerala vs N.M. Thomas AIR 1976 SC490
11. A.B.S.K. Sangh vs Union of India, AIR 1981 SC298
12. K.C. Vasanth Kumar Vs State of Karnataka AIR 1985 SC1495
13. Indra Sawhney vs Union of India AIR 1993
14. Janhit Abhiyan vs Union of India AIR 2022

These landmark judgments serve as a testament to the ongoing dialogue and debate surrounding reservation policies in India. They highlight the importance of continuous evaluation, refinement, and adaptation to ensure that these policies effectively address the needs of marginalized communities while upholding the principles of equality and social justice

79

Conclusion

This extensive journey has equipped us with a wealth of new information and a deeper understanding of reservation across its various facets. Our exploration of reservation has been a rich and extensive journey, equipping us with a profound understanding of this complex concept. We delved into various theories explaining its origin, traced its historical evolution, and examined how caste persists and manifests anew in the modern world. We analyzed who faces the harshest realities of social and economic disadvantage due to caste, and explored the injustices and hardships people suffer from caste-based discrimination. This exploration went further to understand how these discriminatory attitudes have evolved and continue to impact younger generations. We also highlighted the important constitutional framework that guarantees reservation as a fundamental right, aiming to achieve equality through equity. Our journey wasn't complete without a deep dive into the historical context, examining the development of reservation during both the colonial and post-independence eras in India. Also, we focused on the unique case of Tamil Nadu, where the origin and evolution of reservation set it apart from other Indian states. Our exploration of reservation wasn't just about its right or wrongness. We delved deeper, examining its core purpose: uplifting marginalized communities. We debated the continued need for reservation in today's world and considered when it might achieve its ultimate goal. We drew inspiration from the great leaders and contributors who envisioned a socially equal India, free from caste-based discrimination. This vision aligns perfectly with the fundamental human right to equality, which we also explored in detail. The discussion then turned to the concepts of caste abolition and annihilation. We compared community certificates and casteless certificates, ultimately concluding that no document can truly eradicate caste or the discrimination it fosters. It's through human behaviour and a shift in mindsets that we can dismantle this system. The choice lies with each individual: to promote caste and discrimination, or to work towards their abolition. Our exploration encompassed the Economically Weaker Sections (EWS) quota and examined landmark court cases that significantly shaped the evolution of reservation policy. This comprehensive journey aimed to build a nuanced understanding of reservation and dispel common misconceptions.

Equality is a fundamental right, inherent to all living beings on Earth. Discrimination based on factors like caste is not only unjust but also inhumane. As responsible citizens, we have a moral obligation to treat each other with dignity and respect. Affirmative actions like reservation serve to uplift marginalized sections of society by promoting their well-being and social mobility.

Let us strive to cultivate a positive mindset imbued with humanity. Together, we can stand against discrimination and ill-treatment, paving the way for a more just and equitable society.